Contemporary Theatre Studies

A series of books edited by Franc Chamberlain, Nene College, Northampton, UK

Please see the back of this book for other titles in the Contemporary Theatre Studies series

GARDZIENICE

POLISH THEATRE IN TRANSITION

Paul Allain

Goldsmiths College, University of London, UK

Routledge
Taylor & Francis Group

LONDON AND NEW YORK

First published 1997
by Harwood Academic Publishers.
Reprinted 2004
by Routledge,
11 New Fetter Lane, London EC4P 4EE

Transferred to Digital Printing 2004

Copyright © 1997 OPA (Overseas Publishers Association) Amsterdam B.V.
Published in The Netherlands by Harwood Academic Publishers.

British Library Cataloguing in Publication Data

Allain, Paul
  Gardzienice: Polish theatre in transition. – Contemporary
theatre studies; v. 22
  1. Gardzienice   2. Theatre – Poland
  I. Title
  792'.09438

  ISBN 90–5702–106–4

The author wishes to thank Routledge Publishers for permission to reproduce "A
map of the Partitions", which is taken from *A History of Poland* by O. Halecki, 1978.
Every effort has been made to trace all copyright holders; but if any have been
inadvertently overlooked the author will be pleased to make the appropriate
amendments at the first opportunity.

Cover photograph: Anna Zubrzycka-Gołaj talking to *Dziadek*, storyteller and company supporter, in his home in Gardzienice, 1989. Photo: Hugo Glendinning.

CONTENTS

INTRODUCTION TO THE SERIES

Contemporary Theatre Studies is a book series of special interest to everyone involved in theatre. It consists of monographs on influential figures, studies of movements and ideas in theatre, as well as primary material consisting of theatre-related documents, performing editions of plays in English, and English translations of plays from various vital theatre traditions worldwide.

Franc Chamberlain

LIST OF PLATES

(Following page 77)

ACKNOWLEDGEMENTS

I would like to thank my family, friends and colleagues in Britain and in Poland for helping me research this work and knock it into shape. They include Clive Barker, Judie Christie, Barry Edwards, Richard Gough, Alison Hodge, Myles Holland, Marta Kaczuro-Kaczyńska and her family, Joanna Labon, Ken Lubienski, Elizabeth Maslen, Susan Melrose, Katie Mitchell, Helena Reckitt, Maciej and Hania Rychły, Tim Spicer, Nicola Tonks, Agnieszka Wagner, James Wilson, Professor Noel Witts and Grzegorz Żiółkowski. I thank all at Goldsmiths' Drama Department including Robert Gordon, Simon Trussler and above all Professor Vera Gottlieb who supervised this work originally as a thesis. Finally I am immensely grateful to the members and associates of Gardzienice Theatre Association who accepted my intrusions with unquestioning tolerance and affection. Above all, I thank its director, Włodzimierz Staniewski, for making me search further and not letting me rest.

Special thanks to Hugo Glendinning for his photographs and to Rae Smith for her line-drawings.

INTRODUCTION

'I always worked with a wall in front of me — now I need to find a new wall.'[1]
(Tadeusz Kantor – 1990)

This book is a case-study of the Gardzienice Theatre Association of Poland, for which most of the research was conducted from April 1989 to the end of 1993. This was a period of great social and political change in Eastern Europe, symbolised by the fall of the Berlin wall in November 1989. Theatre may respond to certain social needs and may channel public concerns. It was such a relationship which originally meant that Gardzienice's activities engaged a specific community, had a particular performance style and a group ethos which was reflected in their theories. Their work was rooted in contact with a particular audience — initially ethnic minorities in Polish border villages — and their performances were created from folk material gathered in rural areas. The company returned to such remote communities to present performances so that the collection of artistic source material and presentation of product were integrated and simultaneous.

This contact with an audience created a particular performance aesthetic rooted in religious iconography, seemingly dangerous and demanding physicality and complex choral and musical work. Scenography and lighting drew on natural resources such as candles, and the episodic performances were structured around traditional songs and music. The productions grew out of both rural fieldwork and vigorous vocal and body training. As the company have expanded their activities, their audience has broadened and their working processes have adjusted accordingly. This book will look at Gardzienice's evolution from the margins towards the mainstream, and their gradual journey away from Romantic ideals and rural culture. This development is partly attributable to the group's own inevitable progression and increasing world-wide recognition, as they now respond to the demands of international festivals in urban contexts.

Gardzienice's theoretical language has not kept up with these changes. It was inspired by Romanticism, which has now been rejected by many Poles who are searching for values that have no associations with the past. The distance between Gardzienice's explanation of their work and the work itself will be shown

by assessing how Gardzienice initially embraced Bakhtin's examination of carnival and Rabelais.[2] An influential source in the first stages of their existence, it
has an obscure relation to their work today. Bakhtin's theories of carnival depend
on a polarised duality which does not now exist in Polish society — the tension
between the official and the unofficial, the state-sanctioned and the underground.
The often illegal, oppositional existence of many artists was invalidated as soon
as Marxism was no longer the dominant ideology in the Polish political system.
The theatre can be seen to be a sensitive barometer of change, because of its ability to be instantly reactive and because in a crisis it is either looked to as a leading
vehicle for expression or as a quieter place of refuge. Gardzienice are not alone
amongst Polish artists in that they are still searching for the language to locate
their own and society's changes.

In the formerly highly regulated society Gardzienice were, as an Association, a challenging organisational model. Relationships to local and central
authorities have been redefined since 1989. In 1993 they were one of the thirty
companies who received funding from the State through the Ministry of Culture,
a number which was a dramatic reduction from previous years. Their practice is
changing accordingly, becoming more publicly accessible and known in Poland.
Such recognition and development could be considered inevitable as Christopher Innes suggests in *Holy Theatre*:

> *It is the fate of every successful avant-garde to be adopted by the society they despise or
> oppose, to be taught by universities . . . a process of emasculation through which radical
> ideas do act as leaven on the public consciousness, but only at the expense of having
> their original explosive force defused.*[3]

Analysis of the contexts in which Gardzienice operated will show that their activities and philosophies acted less as a 'leaven on the public consciousness' but
rather gave voice to and reflected the widespread yet suppressed subculture.
This then raises the complex question whether their 'original explosive force' has
diminished in light of the fact that the company has now been 'adopted' by Polish
society. It seems too early to answer this question fully.

One prevalent idea in Poland since 1989 is that the arts should be fundamentally economically self-sufficient with minimal State funding. This is in
antithesis to former Communist policies, which promoted active State involvement in and control of culture and the arts. As well as now having to adapt to a
free-market system, the arts are being squeezed by a crippled economy. Firmly
established ideas and modes of practice, such as permanent ensembles, are threatened. Ensembles may survive in the present adverse circumstances, but the very
notion of an ensemble has been challenged by commercial considerations such as
access to well paid jobs abroad and wider possibilities for television work.
Gardzienice are not immune to commercialisation.

One factor which can help in sustaining both a company of people and an ideology and artistic practice is the sense of working in opposition to another set of codes or rules. Oppression can help define creativity and encourage exploration. A conflict could be identified in the early work of Gardzienice — between the group's beliefs and those of the official society in which they existed. However there is now such confusion and turmoil in the transitional period in Poland that this opposition has become blurred. This is to be expected in the unique context of the realignment and total review of the last forty years of European history. Tadeusz Kantor's response to the changes, revealed in the introductory quotation, emphasises the previous clarity from which the present indeterminacy has evolved. The usual initial response to the dissolution of a wall is celebration as happened in Berlin 1989. Realisation of the importance of limitations, boundaries and the possible functions of walls arrives later. In the ensuing confusion there are few points of orientation and a sense of anti-climax follows enjoyment of the immediate gains, as has been the pattern in Eastern Europe.

Artists may be motivated by conflict or can at least manipulate the clearly defined oppositional forms. They can work within and against, or outside of and in contradiction to these, often choosing satire as their means of protest. The Polish essayist, poet and academic, Stanisław Barańczak, who now lives in America, has reluctantly referred to the validity of such opinions:

> Is there any truth after all, in the perverse paradox which holds that creativity can flourish only in the foul air of oppression, whereas a breeze of freedom makes it wither? Being an emigre myself I'd rather dismiss it as a bogus generalisation. As much as I hate to admit it, however, the career of Alexander Zinoviev is a case in point: since his expulsion from the Soviet Union in 1978 he has not written a single book that can stand comparison with his earlier satirical masterpieces.[4]

Kantor is one Polish example from the performance world who affirms Barańczak's question. He described the chaos, destruction and repression of the Second World War as the most fruitful time of his creative life. Images from that period constantly reappeared in and fed his work, such as the wounded soldier 'Odysseus' returning from war. I would not limit by using the word 'only' as Barańczak does, but opposition has been central to the work of many Polish artists as inspiration for creativity. It certainly inspired Gardzienice, particularly in their use of the carnivalesque, to which satire, or at least a highly critical oppositional perspective, is central. It is one common thread which united Polish theatre practitioners with such differing aesthetics as Kantor and Gardzienice. One can more clearly examine the nature of Gardzienice's possible 'emasculation' when it is considered within a frame of vanishing opposition.

Art might thrive on repression but it is not an indispensable stimulant. In a utopian democratic society artists have the possibility to criticise, praise and analyse whoever and whatever they wish with responsibility only to their promoters or audience. They may operate under the banner of so-called 'freedom of speech', yet they face less obvious restrictions than artists in a Communist society endure, such as financial restraints, an interfering sponsor or self-censorship. Many Poles, like Barańczak, crystallise these differences, having worked in Communist and then free-market worlds. Nobel Prize winner Czesław Miłosz made the crossing in 1951 and is now settled in America. He has argued that open societies can impose personal difficulties on artists, which might even make than turn to Communism in order to focus their expression:

> *Westerners and especially Western intellectuals, suffer from a special form of* taedium vitae; *their emotional and intellectual life is dispersed. Everything they think and feel evaporates like steam in an open expanse. Freedom is a burden to them. No conclusions they arrive at are binding: it may be so, then again it may not. The result is a consistent uneasiness. The happiest of them seem to be those who become communists. They live within a wall which they batter themselves against, but which provides them with a resistance that helps them define themselves.*[5]

Miłosz implies that self-definition can grow indirectly from others telling you who you are or should be and what to think. For him artistic expression is inextricably linked to this sense of identity. This may be more true of the solitary nature of writing than it is of the communal activity of theatre. Yet if his assertion is true, then the dilemma for Polish artists now may be that they long for the artistic potential provided wittingly and unwittingly by the former regime. Polish Romanticism found virtue in martyrdom, sacrifice and struggle. 'Freedom of speech' is now an actuality for all Polish artists, but does this serve as a stimulus or a disincentive? The model of Gardzienice in this transition gives us tentative understanding of the differences between making art in both Communist and Capitalist-orientated societies, (or in this instance Capitalism in its earliest stages).

One difficulty in my research was the depth and speed of reconstruction in Poland. By Spring 1993 the country had seen four Prime Ministers in as many years. Some of the trends and developments which I outline began before 1989, the year when I first met Gardzienice and travelled to Poland. However 1989 marks the starting point of a period which politically consolidated and thus allowed an unstoppable chain of radical developments, openness and reassessment. Since then terminology is continually changing, be it street-names or the titles of political parties, as history is redressed and rewritten. Appropriate verb tenses have not come easily in my writing, reflecting this uncertainty and flux. Theatre, as a social activity, is inseparably interwoven with certain periods and contexts, which give it purpose, structures and fundamentally an audience. I examine the historical, social and political shifts in contemporary Poland with the full awareness that these are fast drifting sands, an image which pertains as much to Gardzienice's progression.

As written texts, Gardzienice's performances reveal little and are not included. There is sparse academic writing in English about Gardzienice except two articles by the Polish American academic Halina Filipowicz, a brief section by George Hyde in *European Theatre: 1960–1990* (Ed. Yarrow, 1992) and my own publications. Most of Gardzienice's key philosophical attitudes and statements have been printed in English, this being their second language, though translations are uneven. I have read and collated much unpublished material, including diverse short works and scraps of conversation or statements, gathered by ear, pen and tape recorder, along with quotation from Staniewski himself. There is paltry chronological documentation, which mainly comprises slides, videos, personal accounts and interviews. The most information is in Polish although this is sparse and often descriptive rather than analytical. The company's relationship to critics does not encourage objective research, for Staniewski controls much of the criticism of their work and has close contact with three Polish journalists who have become spokespeople for Gardzienice in Poland.

Most of my research stems from personal contact with the company abroad and in Gardzienice village itself (the company take their name from the small village where they are based). It can prove hard to distance oneself from such a relationship. Information about the company has also been hard to unearth because ultimately the group prioritises action over theorising and the practice over the administration. I have unearthed little detailed information about the company's economic situation. Staniewski side-stepped my requests for this, pointing to the complexity of their finances and doubting how this could be of interest to me. This has resulted in a gap in my research. My study has also inevitably been more objective when considering the early years of the company's existence, in which I took no active part.

Some terms used in this book require clarification, such as the difference between ethnic and national. The former implies a subgroup with its own cultural identity and shared history that exists within a wider dominant ethnographic structure. It is not defined geographically but through blood ties. The larger group within which the smaller exists can often be described as a nation with geographical borders, a common language and heritage. Within this there can be many ethnic subgroups, as is the case in Poland. Gardzienice's emphasis on the Slavic influences in their work shows leanings towards an ethnic rather than national theatre and a rejection of nationalist ideals, as will be clarified.

Another contentious term is tradition. One interpretation which I have found sympathetic for this work is in David Coplan's question that he posits in his essay 'Ethnomusicology and the Meaning of Tradition'. Coplan is pointing to the long arm of cultural manipulation that has touched most corners of the world:

> *Where to find African traditions, not as animated museum pieces, tourist displays, commoditized diversions, instruments of state policy, nor even as conscious reinventions for the creation of a new identity or political ideology, but as organic, living expressions of collective experience in aesthetic form?* [6]

Gardzienice are asking the same question, only in a wider geographical context. Use of this description avoids a lengthy unpicking of its meaning and is helpful for addressing the questions I raise about the relationship between nature, identity and cultural expression. This work will show that the destructive falsifications of Communism have now been replaced by similar dangers in the form of lack of regulation, a fast pace of swinging changes and rampant commercialism. 'Organic' traditions such as those Gardzienice seek and Coplan describes continue to face the threat of external control and distortion.

Chapter One puts Gardzienice's practice in a Polish theatrical context in relation to the specific aesthetic of Romanticism. Chapter Two views the society in which they work and describes Gardzienice village, analysing how this has changed since the company's arrival there. Their relationship to their audience is then assessed in Chapter Three, referring to notions of the carnivalesque and the changing face of social interaction. In Chapter Four their evolution is examined in relation to Grotowski and paratheatre which influenced the practice of the group. This leads on to the heart of this work and analysis of their physical and vocal training in Chapter Five and performances in Chapter Six. The book then broadens its focus. Chapter Seven looks to other possible models to determine Gardzienice's future and Chapter Eight assesses how Gardzienice's work in a reformed society now relates to the politics of cultural exchange, with particular regard to music. By looking at Gardzienice's most recent explanations of their work and Staniewski's search for a new language, Chapter Nine approaches some conclusions about the fast changing relationships between Polish theatre practitioners and their own artistic material as well as their public.

The model of Gardzienice raises the broader question of whether artists can escape or suppress deeply entrenched behavioural patterns in order to respond to quickly evolving external social conditions. If a particular context shaped their style and conventions, breaking away from that pattern may necessitate a loss of identity. If Romanticism does not offer any inspiration to artists in contemporary Poland, how can theories, which need time to distil, follow the speed of practical reforms? Can a future Polish theatre evolve which uses another language within fresh frames of reference? One popular option seems to be to adopt

Western models. These have been attractive yet inconceivable for forty years but might stifle creativity. They collide with philosophies and practical approaches from Eastern cultures, which have deeply influenced the work of companies such as Gardzienice and Grotowski's Laboratory, visible in director/actor relationships, to name one example. Can there be a sustained creative conjunction when 'East meets West' in Poland (to adopt the now cliched phrase), and what are alternatives to the money-making demands of commercialism? Perhaps the future of Polish theatre and Gardzienice might be a hybrid mixture of received contemporary Western values and former Polish theatrical traditions. This may be a solution which preserves an identity and yet which seeks new frames and administrative structures. Such resolutions are essential for the survival of experimental theatre in Poland which seems almost to be facing a crisis of extinction and certainly an identity crisis. This book hopes to clarify some of the more pertinent issues as a partial response to these present difficulties.

1

POLISH THEATRE – ROMANTICISM FADES

An analysis of the predominant trends in the practice of major Polish theatre artists of this century reveals how Gardzienice's work belongs to a particular tradition forged in a specific context. The Romantic movement has provided a theoretical and historical framework for Polish drama as well as giving it texts and mentors. It has also helped create a Polish theatre with specific attributes — post-Second World War alternative theatre in Poland has continually challenged theatrical boundaries and has been internationally recognised for its visual rather than literary means of expression. The content of performances has often opposed the dominant social and political values and ignored the narrow parameters of Communist dictates. This can be seen in a wide range of productions including Gardzienice's which also draw on Romantic aesthetics and Polish theatrical traditions. Gardzienice's performances are visual, physical and metaphorical, evolve from detailed actor training and utilise religious and folk imagery and symbolism. The influence of Romantic ideals on Gardzienice also pertains to wider aspects of their work, including the search for inspiration from nature, the value of folk culture and the importance of journeying to foreign cultures to broaden artistic sensibilities.

The driving political underground force and corresponding aesthetic in Polish culture which Romanticism inspired have both been undermined by the changes after 1989. With the collapse of Communism, a period of dynamic creativity notable for its specific idioms ended. Reflecting the way that political structures have been reconstructed, the Romantic ideals which shaped Polish theatre have faded, affecting the identity and practice of Polish artists in a now transformed Europe.

Romanticism was a major force in shaping Polish identity and national consciousness. The movement of European artists like Byron and Büchner towards Romantic ideals coincided with specific events in Polish history which deeply marked Polish consciousness. Romantic aesthetics (free-will, artistic expression as a vehicle for political change, and the inspirational role of nature and folk culture, to name but three values for Romantic artists) resonated with the political reality, offering a language of liberation which was utilised not only by artists but by all Polish citizens and in particular soldiers. Politically these ideals fuelled self-destruction in the loss of life in the failed uprisings (notably 1863) that shook Poland during the occupation of the Third Partition.[1] However, as the cycle of Liberation and Occupation has been repeated, Romantic aspirations have continued to also create a sense of a united nation in immensely difficult periods of Poland's history.

Artistically, Romanticism built a foundation of works which have been continuously inspirational, though also resulting in introspection and parochialism. It created heroes and mentors who remain important figures today. In the theatre these were Adam Mickiewicz (1798–1855), Juliusz Słowacki (1809–1849), and Zygmunt Krasiński (1812–1859) and even the characters they invented such as Mickiewicz's Konrad. Their plays and poetic dramas form the Polish classical repertoire and have determined the ideology of Polish artists for many years. Their prominence has been due not only to the quality of their writing but also the connection of their content to Polish political history. Their works have been used for political protest as much as theatrical experimentation, showing how closely the Polish Romantic ideals have been rooted in circumstance.

Mickiewicz was the leader of the Polish Romantic movement. As Romantic artists looked to tradition for inspiration, he questioned what Polish and Slavic culture is, almost from an objective perspective; he had been brought up in a dispossessed country, had lived in exile in Russia amongst a hostile people (the Russians and Poles had been enemies for many years) and had eventually settled amongst the exiled community in Paris. His childhood bought him into contact with White Russian and Lithuanian peasants and their folk customs. The structure of his major drama *Dziady/Forefather's Eve* is based on a White Russian rite of ancestor worship. He turned to folk material to describe his own and Poland's identity, a process which he advocated for all Slavic artists:

> Such a drama should be lyrical, and it should remind us of the admirable melodies of popular folk songs. It should at the same time enable us to hear the stories . . . of the Slavs . . . the Serbs . . . the mountaineers of Montenegro . . . To create a drama that could be recognised as national by all classes of the Slavic race . . . it is necessary . . . to cover the entire spectrum from the simple song to the epic.[2]

He wanted to create a national drama and style that would use all theatrical means such as painting and lights, and which was rooted in poetry. Inspiration could be sought in a rural environment:

> The poets should imitate the Slavic storytellers, the Slavic peasants. You are aware that no people have as rich or as marvellous fantastic tales . . . the artistic secret that the peasants, the native poets, possess. They have preserved that most precious quality, that of admiration . . . Above all he admires the word, he admires thoughts and feelings expressed by the word: that is the poetic character of the Slavic people.[3]

Mickiewicz was not proposing a nationalistic expression of art, but that of a people from common ethnic origin; not a Polish but a pan-Slavic one that cut across externally imposed borders. Ultimately this might be for political purposes because of the oppression the Poles then faced, but his prime concern was the search for a sense of belonging — a home and cultural roots — and for the inspiration this can give. One may have to travel a long way and endure exile but the ultimate destination was home.

Reflecting the Romanticists' embrace of lofty verse as their expressive medium, poetry — and drama as the active embodiment of poetry — had a particular political and social function for Mickiewicz. It could awaken people to self-realisation and activity in order to fulfill their capabilities. The oppression of the Third Partition led him to rediscover an identity, a metaphysical territory where there could be self-determination through the arts. By reaching into the Slavic mentality and persona, with its love of the supernatural and respect for the spirit world, one could personally begin to fight the oppression. The efficacy of his own writings had taught him how this could then guide and unite others. The Romantic respect for the metaphysical for him was rooted in the fact that he could not write for an actual stage. Due to the foreign occupation of Polish territory, *Dziady* did not receive its premiere until 1901, seventy years after its conception. Unable to see his works produced, his plays show a vivid imagination and extravagant theatricality, and are peopled with demons and spirits.

The role of the poet/artist for Mickiewicz was that of a *wieszcz* — a seer and visionary — as he himself indeed became. This love of heroism embraced the entire Polish nation in the form of Messianic Romantic nationalism, a concept fostered by all the Romantic artists. Poland was suffering as Christ had, but would rise again to save the world. In *The Books of the Polish Nation and of the Polish Pilgrims* Mickiewicz wrote that 'the nations shall be saved . . . / through the merits of a martyred nation, and they shall be baptised in the name of God and Freedom.'[4] His own suffering and 'pilgrimage' to Paris in the 'Great Emigration'[5] and his intention to thereby save Poland, were a model for the nation which actually existed only in people's hearts and minds for 120 years. With its important geographical position, Poland was considered the Christian watchdog, keeping the pagan forces of the East from the doors of Europe.

Beyond his influence on national and political ideology, Mickiewicz has had an undisputedly formative effect on Polish theatre. Gerould has outlined the significance of Mickiewicz's Slavic lectures, given in Paris in the 1840s, which crystallised his thoughts on Slavic culture:

> *The spirit of modern Polish theatre lives in this prophetic essay by Mickiewicz, surely one of the great documents on theatrical art and a constant impetus to creative work in*

*Poland...Kantor, Grotowski, the Theatre of the Eighth Day, Gardzienice, and all that
is best in modern Polish theatre have helped to realise Mickiewicz's vision of a Slavic
drama of the future which he knew would some day come into being.*[6]

Since Wyspiański's 1901 premiere of *Dziady*, this play has been nearly constantly
in repertoire somewhere in Poland. The Romantic texts have been used not necessarily as complete plays, but have shed their influence in a broader way. They
are valuable for their imagination, debates and poetic style. Many directors use
the structure of *Dziady*, for example, as a starting point, loosely interpreting the
text. It has been popular with the avant-garde to employ such classics as a basic
for experimentation. Sometimes those texts have been reduced to detailed artistic quotations and obscure references, much as Gardzienice did in *Avvakum*, as I
will outline in Chapter Six. To draw out the connections between Gardzienice's
work and Romanticism and traditions of Polish theatre, it is necessary to return
to the time when Poland was once more independent after the First World War.
This will reveal the continuous Romantic threads which have only been broken in
the 1990s.

Juliusz Osterwa (1885–1947) worked between the World Wars and could
be called the grandfather of experimental Polish practice. He believed in theatre
as a spiritual mission for a group of people living and working together in harmony and so created his own ensemble. He ran a studio as well as directing
a professional performing group, the Reduta, and created almost laboratory conditions for his research. The actors all wore the same clothes for training
and there was a monastic austerity and sense of duty in their life and work,
demanding great sacrifices. Performances were mostly of Polish plays (like
Mickiewicz the nature of Polish identity was at the core of his work) and were
followed by discussions with the audience. Training was conducted in
periods separate from rehearsals and would often last twelve hours a day. By
shifting emphasis onto the process as well as the product, Osterwa tried to give
these two elements equal weight, starting a tradition which many such as
Gardzienice continued.

For Osterwa the theatre was to serve the public and not the individual
performers. He was keen to reach isolated audiences and his group travelled
around Poland in a train to provincial and remote areas over fifteen years. The
most notable example of this was his 1927 touring production of *The Constant
Prince*, which points to his influence on Grotowski, who also led provincial tours
of this and other performances. However, Osterwa's importance lies deeper than
the adoption of this model, for Grotowski borrowed Reduta's insignia for his
own laboratory and adapted it slightly in recognition of Osterwa's inspirational
activities. For Grotowski 'Reduta is in our aspirations, our moral tradition',[7] a
tradition which has deep roots in Romanticism. Osterwa has greatly influenced

Polish theatre groups such as Gardzienice. When journeying in the Ukraine in 1993, Staniewski referred often to Osterwa who had also toured to that area when it was in Polish territory before the Second World War.

The Romantic obsession with rural culture was consolidated before the Second World War by several influential Polish directors, who tried to assimilate folklore into the theatre. Painter, playwright and scene-designer Stanisław Wyspiański (1869–1907), author of the Polish classic play *The Wedding* (1901), used folkloric devices to develop theatrical forms and for visual stimulus. Leon Schiller (1887–1954), renowned for his lavish stagings and crowd scenes and his 'monumental' drama, created what he has described as 'song plays' based on folk music. The use of such material in theatrical performances has continued to this day and is particularly evident in the work of Gardzienice. The use of folk symbolism and costumes is just one small strand which led to the evolution of a visually rich performance style.

The central role of fantasy in Romantic dramas laid a foundation of texts inviting imaginative visual interpretations. The emphasis on visual motifs and symbols in Polish theatre this century was developed by contemporary figures such as Kantor, Jerzy Gzegorzewski (b. 1939) and directors of student theatre groups. Some, like Kantor, initially trained as visual artists. Others were simply looking for new forms, creating performances where the scenography was a dominant element. For a few the experience of the Second World War and the Occupation inspired visual designs. Józef Szajna (b. 1922) survived three years in Auschwitz and as a direct result of this he created his painterly style 'Theatre of Catastrophism'. His performances provided a means to purge himself of his experiences and stemmed from a belief that the word had failed and had to be replaced by the image. He was an influential Artistic Director of the *Teatr Ludowy* / People's Theatre of Nowa Huta in Cracow.[8] One of his best known performances is *Replika* (1973, Warsaw), which is still in repertory in Warsaw's *Teatr Studio* today.

The visual nature of post-Second World War experimental theatre has also been attributed to three literary influences — Witold Gombrowicz (1904–1969), Bruno Schulz (1892–1942) and Stanisław Ignacy Witkiewicz[9] or Witkacy for short (1885–1939). These writers' poetic and theatrical style, with visual experimentation and fantasies, oppositional or marginal values and absurd playfulness, was exploited to answer and mock the dry strictures of Communism. Alternative theatres have used these artists' novels, plays and theories extensively, including numerous subtle allusions to their works within performances. The difficulty faced in translating their writings, particularly those of Witkiewicz with his nonsense character names and neologisms, has restricted the international acclaim which these writers deserve. Their localised perspective and their sense of history and experience is specifically attuned to a Polish consciousness which can be impenetrable for outsiders. Their texts have combined with those of the Romantics as sources of inspiration for post-war Polish theatre.

The name of Kantor has been most closely linked to these three. In 1956 he founded Cricot 2[10] theatre company with whom he gained an international reputation, recognised as a leading exponent of European visual theatre with productions like *The Dead Class* (1975). Throughout his life he was at loggerheads with the authorities, being offered and then forced out of academic posts. His theatre pieces stood against all Communist prescriptions, questioning reality, exploring memory and history and using vivid images and metaphors. He challenged assumptions of what theatre is and where it should take place, performing in bombed-out buildings during the war. Kantor died in November 1990 and at his funeral the centre of Cracow was dominated by a procession of thousands and all traffic stopped in the city for two hours. His group still present performances, though the actors now refer to an empty chair where he once sat by the stage. With Kantor's death, Gardzienice's biggest rival in contemporary Polish experimental theatre ceased to exist. It will never be known how he would have developed in the present environment or if he would have found or created a 'new wall' to work against.

During Communist rule, image-based theatre also developed partly as a means to avoid the censors' cuts, hoping to circumvent restrictions with difficult to interpret statements. It is easier to cut words out of a text, for images and symbols prove ambiguous when tone and interpretation can alter their meaning completely. Symbols became a powerful indirect means of expression often as protest, but visual theatre was still accused of collusion with the authorities. With its metaphorical nature and allusions it was seen by some to condone rather than attack the oppressive system. Visual companies such as Kantor's toured abroad and in doing so and in spite of their own independence were considered by some Poles to be a showcase for Communist cultural policies. Yet most international audiences interpreted such Polish productions with political readings that were against the government even if they had subsidised them. The visual language was not necessarily one of collusion as student groups revealed.

The student theatre movement often used non-literary sources mixed with collage techniques. Groups such as *Teatr Ósmego Dnia* (Theatre of the Eighth Day) used series of tableaux mixed with archetypal character-based scenes, a physically energetic style and a parodic tone. This was not just to avoid censorship but grew from a rough and ready, inexperienced way of devising for performance. They presented political and social criticisms openly and payed the price for it, even of physical violence from the authorities. Widely recognised images were distorted as a mockery of the status quo. The Catholic Church and its lavish use of symbols inspired the visual imagination of many Polish directors as did Communist motifs. The student groups could draw on this rich pool when they devised their home-made performances. Many groups toured abroad and the work came to be supported and admired throughout the world. *Teatr Ósmego Dnia* gave highly acclaimed performances at the 1985 Edinburgh Festival, even though some members of the group had not been allowed out of Poland. This company and a few others still exist today and their method of devising performances has inspired many, including the younger generations in Poland whom they are now coaching.

The visual movement in theatre blossomed as a reaction against predominant requirements, which may be termed Kantor's 'wall'. As the anger of 'kitchen-sink' drama erupted in Britain, so a realistic, politically and socially responsible theatre was imposed in Poland. The Socialist Realist movement developed before the Second World War in post-revolutionary Russia. It never took as strong a hold in Poland as it did in the former Soviet Union, Czechoslovakia or Hungary, but it dominated cultural thinking immediately after the Second World War. It described a writing style that was imposed on authors by State-controlled organisations like the Writers' Union[11], yet it also applied to all art forms, controlled by their respective Unions. The State's intentions were to regulate artistic output: to keep art close to the people and accessible to the masses and to make it ideologically correct and socially constructive, according to the Communist Party line. Supervision entailed close analysis and then censorship of anything too critical of government policies. Self-censorship was also encouraged as a means of assessing the extent of an artist's affiliation to the Party. Experimentation was not advised, imagination was not encouraged and uniformity was imposed.

These policies also meant that theatre at this time was hugely subsidised. As part of post-War reconstruction many new theatres were built, opened and renovated over a wide geographical spread. Companies toured to rural areas and puppetry theatres opened. Theatre was to become accessible and available for all ages and all levels of society. Three theatre schools were started and magazines and cultural institutions such as the International Theatre Institute were inaugurated. There were regular national and international festivals, though these excluded Western influences and focused on Soviet playwrights. On average, box office returns would make up a third of a typical regional theatre's budget with the rest from central and local authority subsidy. Actors were assured of receiving a basic salary so over-employment was high. Through this extensive support and encouragement the theatre achieved large audiences and was acclaimed by the authorities for its important role in the development of post-war Communist Poland.

In every case creativity was confined within centrally defined and narrow limits according to 'cultural enlightenment':

> *All activity in People's Poland should contribute to the creation and the development of*
> *a socialist society. Consequently any plays which show a hostile attitude to that principle*

are a priori excluded from the repertory of the Polish theatre. Also rejected are dramatic works which have a harmful effect on culture . . . agencies of the Ministry as well as the regional authorities see to it that these principles are obeyed.[12]

These ethics were as ominous as they sound. Flexible enough to give room to whim and pettiness and powerful enough to offer no compromise, these rules were applied by a large bureaucratic force. Statistics were gathered, scientific analysis made and success was judged by numbers attending, accessibility and the amount of people employed. The favouritism that tainted all political life also filtered into the theatre, with the added attractions of prestigious stars and re-nowned public events. Economic difficulties made corruption rife.

Another aim of the Communist authorities was 'the difficult process of eliminating differences between urban and rural culture and of tracing out a uniform, national road in the field of cultural development.'[13] Cultural forms were encouraged to be conservative and ideologically motivated. Rapid industrialisation was a priority and was reflected by monotonous dramas which set working people in work-related settings and turned them into Socialistic he-roes through simplistic plot developments. The realistic style and the superficial theatrical devices this entailed were nowhere as popular in Poland as in Kazimierz Dejmek's *Teatr Nowy* / New Theatre of the heavily industrial textile town of Lodz. Dejmek's 1949 debut production there of the *Brigade of the Grinder Karhan* by the Czech writer Vasek Kana was typical of this style. For many theatre artists such limitations stifled creativity.

After the Second World War the Romantic dramas were rarely seen until the demise of Stalinism in the mid-fifties. The Ministry of Culture looked unfavourably on these classics for they were often anti-Russian, upheld Christian morals and encouraged non-Communist principles of individualism, all portrayed in a metaphorical style. The Romantic love of nature contradicted rural industrialisation programmes. Slowly de-Stalinisation began to creep into every level of life, particularly in Poland after the death of Stalin in 1953:

In April 1954, the Minister of Culture, Włodzimierz Sokorski, even admitted that 'stag-nation' and 'deterioration' had occurred in the artistic field as the result of the 'false interpretation' of the doctrine of socialist realism.[14]

Laws were further relaxed and restrictions lifted in response to Khrushchev's famous denunciation speech at the 1956 Soviet Party Congress. Channels and access to the West were opened and with this came new inspiration, material and ideologies. *Dziady* was staged for the first time since the war in 1955 by Aleksander Bardini at the Teatr Polski, Warsaw. Its reception was described by Jan Kott:

The production . . . was the most important event in the Polish theatre for ten years. Forefather's Eve struck home with greater force than any play written since the war, in its historical aspect as well as in its contemporary relevance . . . Time did not consume the play's modern spirit, and it still haunts us today. There is dynamite in Forefather's Eve *and it exploded on the first night.*[15]

The play was then produced many times, notably by Grotowski in 1961. Interest in Romanticism and the Romantic dramas thrived, for those plays ideally suited the broad political context at that time with Poland again subservient to Russia.

The repression of the previous years unleashed avid creativity as the underground means of communication and symbolism could be explored to the full. Csato describes this dynamic, innovative time for Polish artists which looked back to Osterwa:

> *While in the period from the thirties to the fifties, the dominating tone in the theatre was a specific brand of realism which tried to maintain a balance between the concrete contents of the picture and its metaphorical implications, now one could observe a concerted effort towards the externalisation of metaphors. Theatrical forms began to grow widely diversified, many of them going back to avant-garde experiments of the twenties.*[16]

This activity grew from frustration, former limitations and severe restrictions. In this new climate could flourish the people and groups and eventually the student movement that made Polish theatre respected all over the world.

The mixture of bold initiatives and ideas with a strong theatrical infrastructure and a receptive public, made fertile ground for theatre practitioners. If subsidy could not be gained from the State, (whereby one could act as society's watchdog through deception and manipulation of the authorities), assistance could be sought from more independent organisations such as student unions, the Church and by the financial consideration that such underground activities were usually well attended. Hard currency could also be gained from touring abroad which could be converted into *złoties* at very favourable exchange rates. This could then support long rehearsal periods.

The peak of theatrical activity declined in the late 1970s and was fully quashed with the imposition of Martial Law in December 1981. In 1977, Gerould detected the end of this golden period, as this remark from *Twentieth Century Avant-Garde Polish Theatre* reveals:

> *This kind of theatre was made at home . . . solely out of an inner need. A genuine personal underground, not a follower of fashion, the Polish avant-garde worked outside the mainstream and apart from the market-place of isms, where styles in drama . . . are soon outmoded . . . Now that Polish avant-garde drama is officially sanctioned, publicly accepted, state-financed and fostered, and as it were mass-produced . . . the Polish avant-garde has joined hands with the Western experimental movements, and now consists of a series of facile, readily available cliches and formulas.*[17]

Gerould locates the peak of Polish theatrical expression in a particular closed, isolated and oppressive climate which inevitably opened up. Increased liberalisation allowed some theatre groups and its makers to tour in the West, inventing a marketable export culture. Yet any form of expression which proves popular and potentially undermining of authority will eventually be adopted by the controlling system, as Innes' quote in my introduction suggested. All these factors led to the decline of experimental theatre in Poland.

With the rise of Solidarity in 1980 the events of daily life were discussed in a public forum and attendance in the State-run theatres fell. Theatre unions supported Solidarity and individuals campaigned in the shipyards, turning their energy to political ends. State theatres were slow to respond to the changes, up against and yet part of the still powerful and slovenly Party mechanisms. However, according to one Polish observer some directors responded seemingly successfully by reorientating theatre:

> Without much rehearsal, gigantic, patriotic, mass spectacles were staged. In Fall 1980 ten thousand spectators gathered in the Katowice Sports Coliseum for a performance based on Kordian and Forefather's Eve. This production and others like it elsewhere were sponsored by Solidarity. Audiences were deeply moved . . . These events were dangerous — for the theatre, for the culture. Theatre again became an object of manipulation, a servant to new elites.[18]

In spite of its cynicism, this comment is important as a balance against the sweeping almost blind feeling of freedom and power induced by the strength of Solidarity. The author recognises the shift in consciousness that came about as being of value yet he is duly wary. This caution seems irrelevant in the light of following events as the already destabilised theatre world was soon completely stifled by the 'State of War', as Martial law is called by the Polish people. During Martial Law, the Romantic plays were still part of directors' repertoires, but not with the same frequency as before, being ousted from popularity by the plays of Witkiewicz.

The reaction of most theatre artists to the military control of the media, the lack of human rights and the widespread arrest of artists, to name but three of the effects of Martial Law, led at first to an informal boycott in particular of the mass media. Independent groups like Theatre of the Eighth Day were ruled out of existence. Many people were sacked, hounded and arrested in what became dangerous times. Travel was greatly restricted and groups like Gardzienice were unable to move around. As theatres then gradually began to reopen, with carefully monitored repertoires, anti-government productions were put on by those clever and determined enough to steer a path through even tighter censorship. They produced matinees when the curfew operated but generally the theatre went deep underground until 1985. Churches became performance sites for directors like Andrzej Wajda. Productions sponsored and hosted by the Church were beyond the jurisdiction of the State and so could criticise it. Private homes were also used for what was called 'Home' theatre, where audiences would arrive at staggered intervals so not to arouse the authorities' suspicions.

The theatre found a sense of purpose in its ability to once again provide a political forum for protest and debate, yet the physical danger and risk killed much of the spirit and desire of people to be creative and to attend cultural events. There was little energy or inspiration for breaking new ground. The use of tired rabble-rousing symbols and productions of the Romantic classics left audiences unstimulated as they became mere artistic vehicles for directors' indulgence. Tanks on the streets, curfew and military rule made people closed in their interaction and restricted in their activities. Oppression, which had previously given stimulus, now defeated many and the circles of public engagement narrowed.

In the latter half of the 1980s, television and video became increasingly popular, as did light entertainment and Western plays. The 'protest plays' of writers like Mickiewicz lost their purpose. After 1989, with Poland wanting to make connections with Western Europe economically and culturally, the classics did not ally with dominant preoccupations. They looked East to the Tsarist and based themselves on national pride and associated Messianic fervour, directed against external forces. With the threat of foreign oppression diminished, many Polish artists now want Polish culture to shake off the criticism of introversion. They are tired of familiar codes and symbols, recognisable only to those with some knowledge of Polish history: the use, for example, of crucifixion imagery to signify Poland's dissection under the Partitions. Izabella Cywińska, former Minister of Culture, is one of those wanting to distance themselves from Romantic idealism:

> *I am not one of those holding a mystical belief in a special mission for Polish culture . . . We left Europe at that very moment when we stopped being universally-minded. And we stopped to be so when we had by necessity to concentrate on ourselves. Professor Leszek Kołakowski describes it as a transition within our mentality from 'the open' to 'the contracted'. It happened at the turn of the eighteenth century when we lost our independence.*[19]

Now the enemy of the director is money and not the censor or Communist pro-Soviet policy makers.

The classics may not be attracting large crowds to the extent that Western farces and musicals are, but there is still a substantial audience for them. Maciej Prus, director of the *Teatr Dramatyczny* in Warsaw has stated that 'We must stop underrating ourselves. We must respect the top romantic dramas of European tradition. Polish theatre is in Europe, in the very center of it. It doesn't have to catch up.'[20] Yet such statements seem built on false vanity. Polish playwrights are not popular abroad and their Romantic plays are rarely performed outside Poland.

What this 'underrating' demonstrates is not so much a permanent rejection of the Romantic dramas but a cultural crisis. It cannot now be assumed that the ideology of those texts reflects the political ideals of the audiences as they once did. Dramas focused on an external oppressor cannot easily be turned towards internal domestic problems and so the Romantic texts do not contain suitable material for the changing Poland. The belief that the country will be the Messianic saviour of the continent seems most inappropriate. The economic crisis is so severe that Poland cannot stabilise itself, let alone lead Europe as a model nation in these financially demanding times. Stability can only come through allying itself with the rest of Europe, opening itself to potential world markets and respecting the controls of bodies such as the International Monetary Fund.

Polish experimental theatre thrived on introversion. Codes and allusions within a narrow framework attacked Communist policies and Romanticism provided images, ideologies and texts for this expression. Now parochialism has been broadly rejected. Openness has allowed free expression and artistic dialogues are no longer only for the initiated. Accessibility and popularity now depend on financial limits. Few are presently embracing the symbols, language and ideals of Romantic fantasy, imagination and escapism in these difficult times. Just as the hardships of Martial Law diluted interest in and support for the theatre, so do present domestic struggles pour cold water on the ideals of Romanticism.

The characteristics of visual theatre I have outlined all went against Communist prescriptions and Socialist Realism. Martial Law has created a barrier and a distance between the heyday of Polish experimental theatre in the early 1970s and the present. Now the free-market system and commercial constraints rule. Tadeusz Bradecki of Cracow has already perceived the crumbling of the notion of an ensemble in his own company at the *Stary Teatr*/Old Theatre. The history of laboratory groups with an emphasis on process rather than product, which can be traced from Osterwa through Grotowski to Gardzienice, will also probably end in the commercially oriented environment, for who will pay for such explorations? Polish groups no longer get favourable profit from touring abroad which previously financed explorations at home and long rehearsal periods. It may be many years before the achievements of the former age are equalled. Poor theatre is once more a fact of artistic life in the 1990s.

2

THE RURAL CONTEXT AND GARDZIENICE VILLAGE

Gardzienice's advocacy of marginal cultures and their choice of a rural base have been inspired by the geographical, ethnic and religious composition of Poland, which has shaped the Polish consciousness as much as has the political history. The company exists in what Staniewski describes as 'active mutuality' with their audience, using the people as animate source material and living and operating within a specific rural setting, which this chapter will outline. Such a group which has an intrinsic connection to its folk culture is unlikely to have been founded in a Western European country. As Poland strives to achieve integration with the West it seems unlikely that such a model will appear again. Native rural culture is already submerged in a process of transformation, perhaps akin to that which has taken place in Gardzienice village itself, where the theatre company has for several years been investing money, much of it made from touring and festivals abroad.

In 1977 Staniewski sought a particular audience and environment as he began to make theatre. Compared to Western Europe, change has been slow in rural Poland in the last hundred years and due to economics and minimal technical progress, the culture of such areas has been little disturbed. These words of a Sioux Indian could as easily describe the village people of eastern Poland:

> *We Sioux spend a lot of time thinking about everyday things which in our mind are mixed up with the spiritual . . . the white man sees so little, he must see with only one eye. We see a lot that you no longer notice . . . you are usually too busy. We try to understand (nature) not with the head but with the heart, and we need no more than a hint to give us the meaning.*[1]

It is such a mentality which Staniewski sought in what he has provocatively called Poland's 'reservations'. A slow rhythm of life, a fusion of the earthly and the spiritual, a physical rather than intellectual perception of the world and a close relationship to symbolism and to nature were all vital for him in his quest for a home and site for his theatre. All pertained to rural Poland, especially in the East.

Staniewski described this area and its people, and his intention in going there in 1977:

> *By going into that space we can bring back to mind and perhaps even revive that magic*
> *quality contained in the root of the word theatre...There is still in Poland a whole*
> *unexplored area of culture, a whole tract, which is now dying, day by day. I am thinking*
> *of that raw, natural native culture...the native culture of Western Europe and of the*
> *United States had died at one time in the name of civilisation and prosperity. That is*
> *the price of progress...Tradition is also dying in Poland.*[2]

The question of how such places and contacts can stimulate theatre was at the core of Gardzienice's research. Staniewski's statement is just about still true today, but the rapid social and economic changes in Poland since 1989 will have a continuing and profound effect on such areas. It is too early to assess the full ramifications of these but some transformations are evident. It seems likely that Polish rural culture will in the near future face a similar demise to that of the 'native culture of Western Europe and of the United States'.

Poland is a vast country with huge tracts of countryside and pine forests worked by farmers and foresters. The far South of Poland is hilly, leading to the high peaks of the Tatras, but the rest of the country comprises the mostly flat and sandy flood plain of the rivers that run from the heights. Vistas are sweeping and open, often showing signs of small-scale cultivation. There are few collective farms, particularly in comparison to former Czechoslovakia and Hungary where agriculture was, until recently, mostly State-run. The land is usually cultivated in feudal plots that are often worked with horses, above all in Eastern Poland.

The further one moves beyond the cities and the financial and industrial centres of Poland, the more prevalent is the poverty. The border area, that connects with White Russia and the Ukraine is described by many as *Kresy*. In Polish this means end or a final line, but it also has other connotations: a place at the end of the world and a region that is dying. These places are literally dying, for the young have left for the towns and cities. These villages could cease to exist within twenty years or less and there are numerous empty dwellings in such places. Schooling has become centralised and is only possible in the bigger population centres. There is no money to finance rural developments or encourage investment, for the infrastructure in such areas is too old and derelict. A reversal of Communist practice — which theoretically wanted to eliminate any economic imbalance between rural and urban regions and industrialise the countryside but which scarcely physically consolidated this ideology — will require substantial financial resources.

Economically, Poland can be divided between East and West, which is reflected in a common 'proverbial' description of the two areas. Poland A lies from the German border to the River Vistula, that runs through the centre of Warsaw. Poland B lies from the east bank of the Vistula to the Russian border. A is rich and B is poor. Clearly a generalisation, this statement is uttered by Poles often with a lighthearted inflection. However, in such sweeping observations there is usually some truth. One can even sense the contrast in wealth and style by crossing from one side of Warsaw to the other, with the Russian Orthodox church dominating the eastern skyline alongside poorer tenement buildings. This gives an indication of the historical facts that lie behind this saying.

Broadly speaking, during the Third Partition of Poland (1795–1918) the eastern area of the country was under Russian domination, the West and North under Prussian rule and the South under Austrian control. The difference between these powers in terms of their wealth and sophistication etched itself on the land. In psychological terms this was reflected by the contrast between the pragmatic logicality of Western European attitudes and the more anarchic spontaneity and impulsiveness of the Byzantine spirit which Poland has always straddled.[3] The East remained badly farmed and the infrastructure was not greatly improved as Russia did not possess the will or the money for such endeavours and concentrated on developments closer to the Russian heartland. In the Prussian sector numerous roads and houses were built and communication lines laid. One can still see the price paid for this inequality: in the contrast between the large corn fields around the wealthy city of Poznan, (closer to Berlin than it is to Warsaw) and the small feudal strips and mixture of crops around the much poorer north-eastern city of Bialystok. There the villages comprise wooden cottages as opposed to the red brick Prussian style in the West.

Gardzienice village lies deep in the countryside in the south-east of Poland, 100 miles from the border with Ukraine. It shares many features with other villages in the region. There is a sparsely stocked shop, no sewage system and most houses rely on drawing water from a well by hand. It has a population of about seven hundred who are nearly all farmers with a small plot of land. They cut hay, have a few cows, chickens and pigs and grow between three and five hectares of wheat or corn.[4] Every cottage has a yard with barns for livestock and crop storage. There was one State-run farm in the village employing about ten people, though this was closed at the end of 1991. The long village is divided into two sections, Gardzienice One and Two, separated by a small stream that runs in the middle of the meadows. There is a primary school in the village that serves a wide radius. The nearest health centre is six kilometres away in Piaski and the doctor's frequent visits to the homes of older people must be relied on for medical support.

Communications in the area are poor, with two private telephones and a public one in the post office. In 1991 Gardzienice had a telephone installed in their theatre space but this can only be used when the post office is open. It normally shuts at three. The technology is archaic and lines are bad. There is a new television aerial nearby so that now both of the Polish programmes are attainable rather than just one as was the case up until 1991. Buses pass through the village roughly six times a day though these are often full and do not always stop.

One unique attribute of the village is the large Folk University housed in a manor house — before the Second World War this was owned by a baron for whom the peasants worked. There are two grand buildings and many signs of former wealth, like the now overgrown, landscaped gardens and extensive chalk wall. Gardzienice rent part of the manor which is an Arian[5] chapel and which was their home and rehearsal space from their early days here. It is not possible for them to buy these rooms with money earnt from touring or international training programmes as they belong to the government. The other baronial building is on long-term lease to Gardzienice from the State. They have only been able to use it since restoration ended in Spring 1991. Staniewski fears it may be taken from them at any point, which would be ironic considering the effort and expenses the company put into its extensive refurbishment. Another village landmark is the wooden mill. It was not working for twenty five years, as millowners had power and independence and were mostly disinherited by the Communist authorities. They did not look favourably on such property owners. As a result there are, throughout Poland, numerous inactive wind and water mills. The one in Gardzienice has been active since February 1992 due to the theatre company's investment of time and money.

Around the village lie acres of open land, forests with sandy tracks weaving through them and small isolated farmsteads. There is a feeling of wildness and poverty in such areas. In the Polish countryside one is always encountering ruins and desolation, be it collapsing mills, schools or houses. There are some examples of State-sponsored industries in such areas, but these do little to alleviate the poverty: 'The south east region, Białystok and the Carpathians are the poorest of all regions, their per capita income is only 85% of the national average.'[6] The Lublin *województwo* or county does not have a high rate of emigration that has affected such areas as the Podhale mountain villages and which has bought in hard currency income on a domestic level. The presence of some rural factories and industries has changed the social fabric to include more 'worker-peasants', as Franklin describes industrial workers who also have their own farm. However, poverty has had a marked effect in preventing cultural and technological advances.

The villagers today are mostly Roman Catholic, though the area has a rich Jewish tradition — before the Second World War approximately 85 percent of the population of Piaski were Hasidic Jews, as portrayed in Isaac Bashevis Singer's novel *The Magician of Lublin*. Few traces of this remain, etched only in the history and mythology of the area and the memories of the older inhabitants. One man in the village has a grindstone which has traces of Hebraic letters on it that was formerly a Jewish gravestone.

The Partitions point to the complexity of Poland's borders and ethnic mixing. The eastern perimeter has often been further to the East and included parts of the Ukraine: before the Third Partition and between the First and Second World Wars to name but two periods. The border with Germany along the Oder-Neisse line was only secured in 1990 through negotiation with Chancellor Kohl. Throughout Poland's history this boundary has moved several times towards the East, almost to Poznan in the fifteenth century. In its central position at the crossroads of Europe, Poland has often been prey to ambitious leaders and hence site of numerous battles. Norman Davies aptly described it as 'God's Playground',[7] the title of his book on Polish history.

Like Spain and Holland, Poland was, for Jews, a relatively safe refuge from persecution by Christians in the Middle Ages.[8] Later, in the sixteenth century, this led to Poland becoming the most important centre of Judaism in the world. This central role in Polish society ended with the Nazi's genocidal aim of 'The Final Solution', put into practice before and during the Second World War. The awful account of the Jews' recent history in Poland is too painfully familiar to recount in detail here, with many concentration camps situated in remote Polish countryside. Some stone synagogues still stand as cultural centres or museums, apart from one in Warsaw which is now open for worship. History lies heavy on the conscience of Polish artists who often use Jewish motifs and artistically explore the relationship between Judaic and Christian culture.

The presence of other minorities in Poland has also diminished, though this is due more to history than genocide. In the fifteenth and sixteenth centuries, when Poland was at its most powerful and expansive in its union with the Grand Duchy of Lithuania, it was known as a 'Centre of Many Nations' — as Staniewski often describes it and as is commonly recognised. Since then, Polish territories have shrunk, usually through aggressive possession. Its multi-ethnic composition has consequently become less diverse. Now only roughly 3.5 percent of the population are of non-Polish origin. Most of these inhabit the marginal regions of Poland. They include 30,000 Lithuanians, 200,000 White Russians, 300,000 Ukrainians (including Lemkos — a separate ethnic group from the Carpathian mountains and an area taking in southern Ukraine) and 300,000 Germans.[9] In the southern mountains there are a few gypsy communities. This mixture arose from distant historical border adjustments as well as more recent ones. The Second World War brought about the biggest migration of European peoples ever, which continued with Stalin's post-war resettlement policies.

The Communist Party's policy was to present an image of a country united in its politics and identity rather than sectionalised as a consequence of history. To generalise, the only divisions the Party encouraged and recognised were between classes and countries — fuel for the working people's war against the capitalist West and the intellectual bourgeoisie, which often depended on anti-Semitism. This was most outspoken in the late 1960s, partly ignited during the Three Day War in the Middle East when many of the Jewish intelligentsia such as Kołakowski were hounded into emigration. Writing about the Soviet Union and the Baltic States, which could easily refer to Poland, Czesław Miłosz described Soviet ambitions in the 1950s:

> *The aim of all these moves is to inter-mix the population of the Union. Only by dissolving individual nationalities in the "Russian Sea" can one attain the goal of a single culture and a single universal language…When the young people learn…how to appreciate all that emanates from the Center, then the Russian language will triumph over all competition.*[10]

Russo-centred, culturally ethnocentric policies strengthened the Soviet Union economically and politically to the detriment of the individual Republics and minority groups. Respect for ethnic identity was sublimated in order to prioritise the seemingly more worthy fight against class and overseas enemies.

Problems of ethnic identity are closely entwined with religion. Poland is predominantly Roman Catholic and has been since 966. The post-Second World War border changes and the extermination of Jews have meant that the number of Roman Catholics has changed from some 60 percent in 1939 to over 90 percent now. There are small numbers of Baptists, Methodists, Lutherans and even Buddhists, to name but a few of the faiths that exist. The small Lithuanian minority is also predominantly Catholic but the White Russians are Russian Orthodox, attached to the Russian church. The Eastern-rite Catholic or Uniate faith practised by Ukrainians and Lemkos is the largest alternative religion to Roman Catholicism. It has looked to Rome for its authority since 1596 and since the Second World War it was consequently encouraged by Russian Communists to rejoin the Russian Orthodox Church, in order to stem Western influences. It has rejected this call and has faced serious repercussions in the Ukraine. A knock-on effect of these Soviet manipulations was that in Poland this religious group were denied legal status until recent legislative changes that were confirmed by a special service led by the Pope in June 1991.

This repression was typical of the Communist Party's anti-religious stance, though in this instance it was connected to suppression of the Ukrainian peoples and their autonomy. Generally the authorities in Poland had an ambivalent relationship to belief in God, so clearly rejected by Marx as an 'opium'. Attitudes were riddled with hypocrisy. In Poland, the long passionate history and sheer breadth of Catholic support prevented the most severe oppression. Various measures were taken to stem the Church's influence, such as disallowing the building of churches but they were built in the secrecy of the night. One symbol of Catholic strength in Poland was the continuous existence of the Catholic University of Lublin (KUL), a focus for dissent. The Church's role as unacknowledged opposition party was heightened by the selection of a Polish Pope, Karol Wojtyla, in 1978.

Within the Catholic Church itself there have been and are many divisions. The peasants tend to be traditionally old-fashioned, as a sociologist's description from 1970 reveals:

> *The Polish peasant is signally religious but religious in a special way. His faith is simple and spontaneous... His private and public religious practices form an integral part of his daily existence... Not impervious to superstition he is more generally apt to adhere to clearly incompatible values.*[11]

Debate among the Christian intelligentsia occurs more frequently in urban areas. Generally there is dissatisfaction with the Church in Poland now as it reveals autocratic tendencies reminiscent of the previous system — for example, forcing every child to study religion in school. The dwindling influence of the Catholic Church in Poland is also attributable to the replacement of spiritual values by material concerns. This is a pattern that most of the Western world has broadly followed with industrialisation and growth from field-based rural societies.

Changes in ethnic and religious rights since 1989 can be detected in one of the most isolated religious minorities in Poland — the Old Believers. This faith was formed as a result of the Great Russian Schism of 1666 and was against the reformist aspirations of Patriarch Nikon. Old Believers split away from the Russian Orthodox Church to preserve traditional elements; most of the men, for example, have beards to align themselves with images of God which depict him bearded. They faced serious persecution because of their rejection of the reforms supported by the Tsar, and many sought sanctuary throughout the world. One of the leading figures of the Old Believer religion, highly active in the Schism, was Archpriest Avvakum (c. 1621–82), who has his own saint's day — 14th April. Gardzienice's third performance is based on his autobiography and even bears his name. Some of this faith settled in the village of Gabowe Grady near Bialystok and the population there are now predominantly Old Believers. Their religion and associated practices and aspects of Russian culture, such as traditional songs and language, have survived intact. This is partly because of their strict religious codes of practice. No singing or playful pastimes are allowed on Saturday and all must take a sauna to purify themselves before Sunday, when there is a service that lasts between three and four hours.

Violence and suppression have followed this minority through history. In Poland some of their few churches have been burnt down by avid Catholics and individuals have suffered physical attacks. As a measure of self-defense and as a response to continual persecution, they are a suspicious and secretive minority. In Russia there are still many supporters of this old faith, though their isolation is as evident there and it is difficult to ascertain their exact number. 'As recently as the 1950s two monasteries and four convents of Old Believers were discovered — for the first time in the present century — in the forests of Siberia.'[12] In Autumn 1992 the Gabowe Grady community organised a large international conference about their religion which was financially supported by the Polish government. This would have been inconceivable before 1989 and proves how the situation has now changed even for one of the most secretive religious groups in Poland.

Nationalist and minority groups' aspirations can now be pursued openly with often chaotic legislative freedoms and with fierce vigour in response to previous suppression. Since 1989 many more forums have become available to discuss Jewish history in Poland. Jewish students produce a regular Jewish newspaper in Polish and the fiftieth anniversary of the Jewish uprising focused world attention on this previously suppressed subject. The situation for other ethnic minorities in Poland is slowly improving as they form their own cultural, social and political organisations. Political representation at a high level is still limited but the new Polish governments have been trying to redress the past neglect by encouraging parliamentary representation for minorities and a parliamentary committee is concerned primarily with their needs. The history of anti-Semitism has made racism a particularly sensitive issue. Polish governments do not wish to be viewed negatively by the international community on whom they rely for financial support. They therefore try to avoid racist policy-making, fighting against history.

The benefits of political reform are undermined by increasing incidents of individual racism as well as international tensions. The Lithuanian minority is claiming that the north-eastern area which they inhabit should be returned to Lithuania as it was theirs in the sixteenth century. The Poles counter this with claims about more recent border arrangements and divert attention instead to the maltreatment of the large Polish community in southern Lithuania. Old rivalries are deep and bitter but there are positive aspects of the recent reforms. There is now a readiness to debate the rights of ethnic minorities. The prejudice that this then exposes might only be countered by long term educational programmes, such as are happening in schools in former East Germany to combat the surge in popularity of neo-nazi groups and where intolerance has its own disturbing associations. Old conflicts might take time to heal, but there have been fundamental shifts in government policies away from ethnocentricity.

The redressed position of ethnic groups does not pertain to Gardzienice village with its Roman Catholic Polish population, but other changes have had a major impact. Until approximately the early 1980s, women used to gather by a cross at six o' clock in the evening to sing hymns. The strength of the religious culture of the village continues to steadily decline. The theatre company's activities have effected the village, (though this is difficult to quantify) giving it both international status and visitors. This has inevitably focused interest on the area and brought some investment (casual occasional employment for local people, to cite one example) and transformed the psyche of many of the villagers, who are aware that the name 'Gardzienice' travels the world. This was exacerbated by the company establishing their theatre centre in the *oficyna*, which began to be realised fully in May 1991.

One cannot predict how the area around Gardzienice will develop but certainly the village's native culture is markedly different from when Staniewski first arrived. Rural areas now share many more features with cities as is familiar in the West. One occasionally sees satellite dishes on the sides of wooden cottages. Both the assertion of minorities through political structures and the repatriation of many people have affected the Polish countryside. However, the changes of the last decade of this millenium will be more all encompassing than those which have happened since the end of the Second World War. Whilst on some levels manipulating rural culture — visible in educational programmes and control of folk arts — Communism suppressed and fossilised it. Oppressive policies, corruption and economic stagnation moulded a passive village population, whom Gardzienice set out to provoke into action.

3

POLISH SOCIETY – THE ART OF GATHERING

Gardzienice's practice is shaped by a particular relationship to their audience. Their rural activities of Expeditions and Gatherings initially seemed to answer social needs for self-expression and public interaction that grew from the restrictions of Communism. Now cultural activities are less limited and not controlled by parameters of Communist policy. These changes have evolved alongside increased influences from the West and reassessment on an international, a European and a more localised level. Theoretical notions of carnival provide a bridge between theatre and Polish society and give Gardzienice's activities a political frame of reference.

People's participation in celebrations and public rituals in the post-Second World War period were always orchestrated by the Polish Communist authorities. The most famous of these were the May Day celebrations with their displays of military hardware. The result of such policies on a social level was empty Culture Houses and disinterest in official cultural activities because of a lack of trust of the authorities and their manipulative aims. Communist ideology broke down on a practical, personal level, as Anne White has highlighted: 'Mass culture is under the control of the Communist authorities. The Communist authorities do not enjoy the society's trust.'[1] The result was that 'Many refuse to take advantage of increased cultural facilities because they do not wish to be socialised by the regime'.[2] Yet outside of Culture Houses, group meetings were limited by both the lack of space and the unwanted attention of the police or Party zealots.

In *Polish Paradoxes* Janine Wedel has an essay titled 'The Ties that Bind in Polish Society'.[3] In this she cites numerous instances of unofficial, 'informal' social activities and the widespread use of networks of family and friends to gain material items such as freezers as well as for personal interaction. This has roots in the Second World War:

> The recent history of Poland is unusually characterised by an unqualified refusal to allow assertive citizens to congregate against the state. The Nazi conquest of 1939 and the Soviet 'liberation' of 1945 shared one crucial factor — an intense hostility to, and suspicion of, any but the most necessary gatherings.[4]

This led to the functioning of alternative networks. Kolankiewicz and Lewis have noted how these two differing worlds have been dubbed *pays légal* and *pays réel*.[5] Subcultural groups and frameworks — part of people's 'second life' as this duplicity has also been known — offered constant resistance to the authorities. When Solidarity, the public face of this subculture, was banned in October 1982 and membership made illegal, the *pays réel* became a sorrowful but active place of refuge:

> *Life of the spirit is carried on in one's own* srodowiska *[circle] and provides the emotional and spiritual fibre of the private world. At small gatherings people share their predicaments, telling stories about their own and others' experiences.*[6]

People hid themselves away, looking for forums of communication and socialisation which empowered them and which they could control. There were few opportunities to meet on a scale between small social gatherings and State-organised rallies.

The organisation that responded to this mutual lack of trust, encouraged public meetings and provided some spiritual nourishment during Communist rule was the Church. Ninety-five percent of Poles were baptismally Catholic (1987)[7] if not actually practising. Just before and during Martial Law, the Church became particularly active, above all at St Brigit's church in Gdansk where Wałęsa spoke regularly to vast crowds during the 1981 shipyard strikes and where he met Mrs Thatcher. As well as providing meeting places, the Church directly encouraged and sponsored artists, especially those sacked or put in prison during the first half of the 1980s.[8] However, such support was mainly confined to cities and large towns. It also did not come without expecting certain commitments to the mission of Catholicism in return, involving both manipulation and sloganeering. For some the Church was not so different from the state in terms of its size, influence and single-minded ideology and politicising, as well as the impersonal collective structures of its religious services and meetings. Its aesthetics were limited to Romantic, religio-symbolic, martyristic and nationalistic imagery and conceptions, and it was a very partial sponsor.

The need for small meetings and informal gatherings outside of State jurisdiction seem in part to be addressed by paratheatre and by Gardzienice's activities, though obviously on a small localised scale. Staniewski was not however looking to redress society's ills (to what extent Grotowski was doing this with his 'Active Culture' programme is more debatable) but to find an audience and a place in which to situate his theatrical activities. His was not a mission of social engineering or political campaigning but an artistic quest. The writings of Mikhail Bakhtin (1895–1975) on carnival brought art and society together with a clear and dynamic analysis.

Staniewski was deeply inspired by Bakhtin's notions of carnival and the carnivalesque as detailed in *Rabelais and his World* and this book became central to Gardzienice's work. This interest in Bakhtin's writings on Rabelais partly stemmed from a reaction against the State's cultural manipulations and an attempt to redefine the notion of 'folk'. Staniewski prefers the word 'native', for the word folk was appropriated and controlled for the State's activities and ideologies. Staniewski's language has a sarcastic tone:

> In Poland a lot of money is poured into folk art, a top priority in the Polish cultural policy. There is a whole army of instructors teaching tradition to rural people. Small wonder that folk art has conformed to what the city wants to see.[9]

Staniewski was searching for places where oral culture, superstitions and native expression still existed relatively untainted and minimally affected by centralised directives.

The battle of Communism against Romantic ideals like Staniewski's had led to radical intervention in the countryside in the name of industrialisation and progress. Folk groups travelled around the world to festivals where their art was judged in competitions. A mild anaesthetised version of rural life was commonly depicted by Communist authorities through its folk arts. They became part of a sanitised export culture presenting the homely values of village life in Communist countries that belied the actual corruption and poverty. Artistic means were used to create a disjunction between real life and representation. Staniewski's term 'native' was in opposition to the word 'folk' and all its implications. His acknowledgement of Bakhtin's ideas could help redefine terms of social engagement outside of Communist parameters, within the *pays réel*.

Bakhtin's theories of carnival related to the Polish context on several levels and helped to relate the theatre practice of Gardzienice to the political context. In *Rabelais and his World* Bakhtin underlines the dualities present in carnival as he describes how folk culture was celebrated on certain days called carnivals, a mediaeval form of folk expression within a definite time-scale. Even the uncertain etymology of the word shows a duality, stemming either from *Carne vale*, Latin for 'meat farewell', or from *Carnem lavere*, Latin for 'to put away meat'. It described the indulgent period before abstemious Lent in the Catholic calendar. The contrast between the two periods, the complete swing from one extreme to the other, is graphically portrayed is Brueghel's picture 'The battle between carnival and Lent.' Battle is a central image of carnival, representing two conflicting attitudes or priorities. From a human perspective the contrast between the two extremes implies a daily struggle, the clash between desire and restraint, broadly resonant of life in Communist Poland.

From a notion of carnival comes the adjective 'carnivalesque' describing features peculiar to such festivities, though perhaps outside of the rigid time base which originally defined the word. It is a useful extension of the notion of carnival and one that can cover many aspects, as Stallybrass and White stress:

> *If we treat the carnivalesque as an instance of a wider phenomenon of transgression we move beyond Bakhtin's troublesome folkloric approach to a political anthropology of binary extremism in class society ... it reveals that the underlying structural features of carnival operate far beyond the strict confines of popular festivity.*[10]

What made elemental folk activities carnivalesque for Bakhtin and the concept relevant to the Polish context and Staniewski is the relation of the carnivalesque to more formalised structures of expression. Carnival as a chaotic time of free will and the carnivalesque as a description of unruly celebrations with their associated images and language, only exist in response to a lack of freedom. The nature of carnival is a momentary suspension of official everyday rules:

> *Bakhtin's use of carnival centres upon its doubleness...there is no unofficial expression without a prior official one or its possibility. Hence in Bakhtin's analysis of carnival, the official and unofficial are locked together.*[11]

In my analysis, the words carnival and carnivalesque are employed for their political and folkloric connotations, always implying a dominant culture and vivid if not suppressed subculture.

Bakhtin saw immense value in these Dionysian times of protest and volatility and saw strength in the people's search for truth and their free-ranging expression of desires. For him carnivals had positive regenerative qualities and were important as a continuing development of folk activities. He analysed Rabelais as someone who

> *continually used the traditional folklore method of contrast, the 'inside out', the 'positive negation'. He made the top and the bottom change places, intentionally mixed the hierarchical levels in order to discover the core of the object's concrete reality.*[12]

Carnivals were initially the people's and not the authorities' property, allowing an honesty of expression outside of political and social constraints. Yet Bakhtin describes how the historical progress of folk culture has been manipulated and politically controlled through the adoption of its forms. Such control was partly as a response to the threat which folk expression has always posed:

> *For thousands of years the people have used these festive comic images to express their criticism, their deep distrust of official truth and their highest hopes and aspirations.*[13]

For Bakhtin the inversion of roles and temporary displacement of authority showed a vibrant desire for liberty and self-rule. For Staniewski the revitalisation of carnival had artistic potential and was a response to Communist control of folk culture.

Bakhtin's history shares some elements with Gardzienice's existence, notably in the connection between expression and isolation. His exile to Kazakhstan and Odessa, on margins distant from centralised Stalinist control, became the only possible means by which he could pursue his interest in language and his belief in the power of people against an imposed ideology. *Rabelais and his World* reveals a subtle Aesopian criticism of the Stalinist Socialist Realist philosophies in its counterideology and admiration of satire. Bakhtin analysed the true, deep belly laugh as capable of undermining the established order and empowering the underdog. He lived in a fearful society, where one had limited choices: obey or face life-threatening consequences, or isolate oneself to avoid unsolicited interest. Bakhtin survived by the latter option much as Gardzienice did in a small isolated village. One can understand the importance of Bakhtin and his ideas for the company in that context and the strong connection of his writing to the dual worlds of Polish society.

Reconnaissance, Gatherings and Expeditions

Born in the Polish countryside, Staniewski returned there to rediscover the impulsive spirit of celebration and to stimulate his theatrical explorations amongst an open audience. Old people, unfamiliar with live theatre or perhaps never having witnessed any, would hopefully react openly and honestly to his performances. They were familiar with story-telling and religious rituals and rites of passage, but would scarcely have seen complex theatre like Gardzienice's. For Staniewski these people possessed intangible though stimulating qualities:

> We are working in those cultural enclaves that have been sentenced to be exterminated . . . For our first performances we invited the old people — with the knowledge that they represent a world that is going away . . . we believe that a human being on the threshold has much more to say than one who is in the middle . . . they gain an enlightenment, a fullness.[14]

Staniewski said that his group wanted "to travel to places that are the end of the world" not in a search for a "singular truth" but "scattered pieces of it found in actions and beliefs of each individual."[15] Eastern Poland offered this. The company therefore organised Expeditions to rural areas which became a time of carnival — a microcosmic existence separated from the everyday, with its own laws, priorities and forms. They used the carnival's images, objectives and anti-structures in a practical way, recognising how its philosophical frames embraced their marginal oppositional stance.

Before Martial Law placed restrictions on travel, Expeditions were undertaken regularly by Gardzienice, almost once a month. They demanded minimal expense and drew partly on company members' private money and the hospitality of their host communities in terms of accommodation and even sometimes basic foodstuffs. Each would last several days and varied considerably in personnel and form. Expeditions have been described by Staniewski as a

> *series of open-air activities, arranged according to a scenario. Wanderings, meetings,*
> *exercises, rehearsals, performances, gatherings. A way of acquiring material for perfor*
> *mances and verifying its initial shape...Harmonising theatrical activities with the*
> *sculpture of the earth's surface and the colour of human settlements.*[16]

They are in part an extension of Gardzienice's daily practice in an unfamiliar environment, though the travel to such places is a key part of Expeditions. Journeying is at their heart, involving complex organisation as well as physical effort and commitment. The travel encourages an openness to what may come and prevents anticipation, almost becoming a model of rehearsal. Analysis of the metaphor of performing as a journey is too familiar to enter into here, notable in the work of Grotowski to name just one example. On a practical level the journeys create their own rhythms and needs, demanding co-operation and flexibility and helping to establish a group's identity.

Expeditions would usually be preceded by Reconnaissance. This is a fact-finding mission by a small group to research a particular community's native culture and to establish if a place has any desire to host the company. If it is deemed to do so the small vanguard must prepare the practicalities for the arrival of a larger group at a later date. Musical material that is gathered on Reconnaissance can then be learnt and used on the Expedition, so that participants are prepared for the encounters. This research is done with exacting and necessary precision, for the Expeditions usually happen in harsh terrain and under difficult conditions.

At the core of Expeditions are Gatherings or meetings with local people. Gardzienice only ever create 'carnivals' in the strict sense of a contained time of festivity during such Gatherings, though these are rarely linked to specific calendrical dates. Through these they aim to provoke cultural activities like singing. Staniewski has described their purpose:

> *Gatherings are the basic form of Gardzienice's artistic practice...the natural background*
> *of theatrical art with its own social framework and social functioning. A fulfilling fes*
> *tivity, having purely artistic aspect as well...so that they can reveal, 'give from themselves'*
> *the truth of the cultural and human existence of their society ...'awakening' the cul*
> *tural undercurrents of a given social enclave.*[17]

Gatherings may have long-term effects over and above the momentary impact of the direct contact, just as ramifications of carnivals spread beyond the time in which they happen. Through Gardzienice's provocation and stimulus, old ghosts and traditions may be recalled and reenacted and these might even reenter the life of a community.

It is of minimal value to describe several Expeditions, Gatherings or Reconnaissances for these are so variable and are as much about each village, personal experiences and daily living, as they are about theatre. Expeditions exist on the border between life and art. Information can be gained from reading accounts by objective observers who have been on Expeditions, such as Osiński.[18] Yet some light may be shed on these processes by my own experiences. The specific nature of the village culture, traditions and rituals in relation to ethnic identity was clarified for me by touring to Polish villages according to Gardzienice's model of practice, visiting places where they had formerly been.

All of the communities I visited in 1991 have long complex histories and varying degrees of politicisation. Some groups, like the Lithuanians, revealed a pressing desire for autonomy and self-determination and impressed their patriotism on us. Others were not interested in the expression of their cultural identity for nationalistic objectives, like the White Russians, who readily described themselves as Poles. Generally, ethnic and geographical isolation encouraged expression of cultural identity. Traditional practices have survived and been sustained owing to numerous factors, though most often they exist not for objective political reasons but as an integral part of everyday life, rooted in religious observance.

On our tour, (organised in collaboration with Gardzienice with young Polish and British actors) our main contact in the villages was with older people. They sing not in official choirs but more as religiously motivated groups, perhaps singing in a local church choir or in someone's house on holy days. I met one such group of Orthodox White Russian women in Knyszewice during *Post*/Lent in the local mayor's house, as part of our Reconnaissance. They sang only hymns — forbidden during Lent to sing folk songs of which they knew hundreds — but invited me back after Lent to hear the rest of their repertoire on our Expedition. In such places people follow calendrical rituals and mark the seasons and oral means are the dominant form of artistic expression. Carnival's temporal structures operate, as does the duality of restraint and indulgence, as religious respect is replaced by the freer spirit of carnivalesque self-expression after or before Lent.

During our Expedition almost the whole village would attend our evening Gatherings which would turn into exchange of songs and dances. People's hospitality and openness were overwhelming as we adapted to the rural rhythm where there was time to stop and listen. There was spontaneity in our meetings which always followed a fluctuating, uncertain course. The songs we heard in return for our presentation usually came from at least before the Second World

War and were sung with vigour. The respect shown to the local singers was invariably extended to us.

Our encounters taught us that people do still meet together and honour their folk traditions. Stimulation and a purpose such as we provided help inspire activity, but there are times of the year such as religious days and events like funerals, weddings and births which are always observed with rituals and song. The main event in the Russian Orthodox calendar is a pilgrimage to the holy hill at Grabarka in eastern Poland. Here there is a monastery, the building site of a new church (the wooden one burnt down), a cemetery and hundreds of crosses that are brought by pilgrims to be planted at the shrine with a prayer. This pilgrimage takes place in late summer and involves thousands of people from all over Poland, who crawl up the hill on their knees in homage. They attain an intensity of emotion and a heightened state of religious fervour. An observer noted how at a Mystery play given during the Catholic pilgrimage at Kalwaria Zebrzydowska the audience "do not merely watch it unfold before them; they relive the events with their minds, their emotions — indeed their whole bodies".[19] Participants attend ceremonies which are an integral part of their lives, which take them beyond everyday activities onto a level of higher spiritual awareness, often induced through physical exertion, be it walking or singing. Assertion of identity is achieved through religious and artistic practices, which exist on both a daily and a more rarified level. Even simple actions such as the singing of folk songs or dancing put people in touch with their ancestors and their history. This is true for Poland's religious minorities as much as for the Catholics.

In such contexts one can understand the functions of Gatherings, as barriers between audience and actors break down and spontaneous expression occurs. With no structured time to finish, they might perhaps last well into the morning, sometimes involving elements of performances and training, food and drink, and only occasionally alcohol. A true sense of carnival is created with no regard for daily distinctions, hierarchies and rules. The oldest people, who might be treated as a liability with little to offer a village community, become the important guests with a very rich cultural memory to offer. Mercantile values are overturned, replaced by cultural ones. Everyone is empowered, held back only by their shyness in a practical realisation of Bakhtin's description:

> Carnival does not know footlights, in the sense that it does not acknowledge any distinction between actors and spectators. Footlights would destroy a carnival, as the absence of footlights would destroy a theatrical performance. Carnival is not a spectacle seen by the people; they live in it, and everyone participates because its very idea embraces all the people.[20]

With few preconceptions of theatre, the 'audience' respond to a Gathering with physical engagement rather than intellectual distance. When we consider the identity of the people Gardzienice choose to work with more closely, we see that encouraging such liberation from everyday values can be construed as having political ramifications, as carnivals may have.

Gardzienice choose to emphasise the cultural values of these meetings rather than the encouragement of political identity, though the two are inseparable. One should not underestimate their political and social importance. A group — Jacek Weksler's *Teatr Wędrujący*/ Travelling Theatre — was even set up by the authorities to officially replicate Gardzienice's activities, though it did not survive long. These meetings perhaps went some way to fill the gap between huge public events and smaller family or friendly social meetings, that Nowak described as the 'social vacuum'.[21] In Poland, Gardzienice usually made Expeditions to ethnic or religious minorities who had been displaced, marginalised or suppressed and who had little political power and social status — groups like the Old Believers. In their Expedition to work with Lapplanders in 1982, Gardzienice encountered another group who have been marginalised and who are seeking political and ethnic status. Gardzienice's rural activities assumed a political, anti-authoritarian nature by working with such people on the periphery of society. They swam against the common tide of feeling, be it a nation's mood or centralised political directives. In Gatherings they encouraged active expression of identity in an open and spontaneous forum, which may provoke declarations of political and social grievances. This may be through direct verbal means or by more embedded cultural forms. Although this is not direct incitement of the people to political action, it could be considered instrumental in arousing political self-awareness.

Gardzienice also went to remote peoples to receive as much as to encourage and to shape their theatre in an energising, stimulating environment. By observation in the countryside the actors acquired a new physical and vocal language, as Gołaj noted:

> *If you confront yourself with people this tells you something about your own culture, traditions and work... new sources of energy, breaking artificial barriers that exist in actors... like looking in the mirror with other people.*[22]

Gadzienice are looking for human experience in the 'university' of the countryside, as Staniewski calls it, and are not asking the people to fulfill expected potential. They demand no formulae and discourage falsity when they encounter it. The essence of carnival is that anyone can take control as may happen in rural Gatherings. Gardzienice are also not looking to preserve what they find as though in a museum, but to challenge and provoke what they encounter into new life according to the regenerative potential of carnival. By following instinct rather than ideologies they are open to non-absolutist structures and human variety and creativity.

Gardzienice's Gatherings now take place more frequently in urban settings and in such a context few elements of spontaneous carnival remain. I have attended them in Britain in 1989, Italy in 1990 and in Gardzienice itself. All these have been with sophisticated, urban audiences and proved to have limited artistic potential. People were introduced to Staniewski's thoughts on culture and the village of Gardzienice through slides, and practical demonstrations of training were sometimes given. A film of the Russian Orthodox rituals at Grabarka was usually screened, clarifying the religious practices which shaped and formed their performance *Avvakum*. (During the creation of this performance there were Expeditions to this holy hill for research during the summer pilgrimage.) The audience were also often invited to be active in what could be called audience participation. In Italy this involved simple singing and attempts at Gardzienice's exercises. In Britain people were invited to spin, a Jewish Hasidic traditional dance similar to the movement of whirling dervishes. Tea was offered and in the village of Gardzienice, where there is a 'Gathering cottage' with cooking facilities, Polish pierogis (potato dumplings) were served before the performance.

There is always a typical format and methodology for urban Gatherings. They act as a preliminary phase lasting between forty minutes and one hour and prepare the audience for the following production. Candles and live music, (usually a flute or *cymbały* — a Polish dulcimer) create a relaxed atmosphere. A carpet designates the performance area (during Peter Brook's 1972 tour of rural Africa a carpet also defined the stage area), and benches and cushions denote the audience's space. The theatrical borders are delineated and participation comes only from being invited over the threshold. There is little room for spontaneity and the hierarchy and distinction between the actors and audience is barely broken down. Artistic assumptions may be challenged by the event but the form within the meeting itself is reactionary, preserving and reinforcing artistic boundaries.

Staniewski is fully aware of the shortcomings of Gatherings in such urban situations. As a minor remedy the 'closeness effect' between the audience members and the actors is used to try to break down inhibitions, but the purpose this physical intimacy and contact serves is minimal. Staniewski wants to foster active participation by breaking down the actor/audience divide and removing the 'footlights'. However the 'closeness effect' cannot enable this alone whilst other restrictions remain. Gardzienice, and particularly Staniewski, control the proceedings with playful but authoritarian enthusiasm. Perceptions of theatrical activity are broadened but this is perhaps as much as can be achieved in such situations. This has value but does not begin to approach the full potential of rural Gatherings.

The central purpose of Gatherings are being called into question by Gardzienice's gradual move away from their original audience. It is hard to find a suitable tense for verbs which relate to the company's practice, with them caught on the cusp between previous embedded habits and fresh perspectives. The development of their Gatherings, which now exist almost in two distinct versions and with urban Gatherings more frequent than rural ones, shows how much original structures have changed. Yet since the beginning of 1991, when *Avvakum* and *Carmina Burana* have been presented as a double-bill, there have been few Gatherings with the performances, particularly on tour. In Gardzienice village, tea is now offered in the *oficyna* rather than in the Gathering cottage and there is no structured pre-performance meeting beyond the grouping of the audience and the anticipatory wait for dusk when the performance begins. Occasionally there is a very brief verbal invitation from Staniewski. The work is not contextualised and there is no longer the transitional walk across the meadows from the Gathering cottage to the performance space: a journey which served to focus the audience and distance them from everyday preoccupations.

Political and social changes have also confined former ideas to history. Radically realigned international relations and new possibilities of travel have made substantial tangible differences to daily life in Poland. Western culture and artefacts have moved from a marginalised though fetishised position to become easily accessible. Before the end of the century Poland may become a member of the European Economic Community. With demonopolisation, participation in the private sector brought concrete personal realisation of the extent of the changes. At the end of 1992, 60 percent of people were employed in private businesses, including agriculture.[23]

With the initial shift of power from the Communists in the 1980s, an important element of social behaviour altered: the notion of collective activity. Poles used to take the side of the satirist in opposition to the closed demands of the controlling authorities. Through the devices of parody and self-mockery individual actions and new perspectives were gradually encouraged. Public events which allowed such self-expression began to be organised more frequently from 1987 onwards by groups like the Orange Alternative Movement and environmental protest groups:

> The credibility of the State and the Party with their orchestrated May Day parades and rallies were undermined by manoeuvres that both parodied them and reminded those in power that civil society could mobilise itself at very short notice on a mass scale ... Alternative models of collective behaviour to the empty rituals favoured by the socialist State or even the processions and open-air masses of the confident Catholic church.[24]

These were absurd demonstrations that would disarm the militia[25] by their lack of political aim and practical intention. People dressed up as 'Smurfs' in mock police uniforms would take the role of police and direct people across empty roads, as they stood obediently waiting for the red light on the pedestrian crossings to change to green. These groups imitated the State and Church but heightened the parody to a sense of ridiculousness and pointlessness.

Such anti-authoritarian activities showed a shift in people's mentality. According to a Polish film critic in 1989:

> *Action is a new category in the Polish culture. It is activity that can make our nation function as a society. The revision of the category of work that has been made weedy by Stalinism ... this re-interpretation has been performed through the idea of solidarity.*[26]

Skwara's essay reveals how Communist cultural policies disabled activity by demanding strictures and a closed methodology of Cultural Enlightenment, which Gardzienice reacted against. Organisations like Solidarity showed the possibility of action from a small-scale level to the huge shipyard protests. Martial Law's repression was fierce but only temporary. A divided distrustful people recreated their collective identity and could express criticisms in public. An environment was eventually forged where an electrician could become a national spokesman and President. This potential was then realised with a democratically elected government and a free-market economy.

This shift which Skwara notes revealed itself concretely after the 1989 Round Table talks. May Day celebrations were replaced by religious celebrations and days marking historic and previously ignored events. One such is the yearly memorial of the Katyn massacre, until recently purposefully and wrongly attributed by Poland's Communist authorities to Nazi rather than Soviet troops — only in October 1992 was blame officially accepted by Russia's government. People are creating new rituals and rediscovering suppressed ones, rewriting social patterns and attitudes that dominated for forty-five years. They are turning to long neglected issues such as Poland's pollution but the irony is that there is no money to support their efforts. If the strong will for change is frustrated because of further economic decline, resentment and bitterness could override the new optimism. The vote in the 1991 elections which was split between so many parties, points to the difficulties that lie ahead.

The social need which Gardzienice's work addressed is no longer prevalent since the collapse of Communist ideology. The desire for periods in which hierarchies could be questioned and redefined, and the search for expression through embracing carnivalesque forms have both been superseded by political and social reforms. Ironically, the redefinition of activity that Gardzienice espoused has overtaken their efforts and disempowered them. People congregate whenever, wherever and for whatever purpose they wish, to assert themselves, share problems and more frequently to trade goods. Social circles are no longer limited by Party affiliations and guidelines. Stagnation has been replaced by fruition as Skwara pointed out. The ethics of a company such as Gardzienice, which in developing the premises of paratheatre encouraged communal co-operation and prioritised cultural expression, have been superseded by principles of materialism and individualism. Activity may have been reclaimed by the Polish people, yet one wonders if the former balance between State-controlled and underground expression allowed a more supportive and fruitful environment for artists and those unable to push themselves forward in a competitive commercial domain.

4

THE FORMATION OF GARDZIENICE – FROM GROTOWSKI AND PARATHEATRE

The theatrical impetus which led to Gardzienice's foundation needs to be examined more specifically and located in a historical context. Their training, for example, was particularly influenced by Staniewski's collaboration with Jerzy Grotowski. Public participation and activity were two prerequisites of Grotowski's explorations, drawing primarily on innate expression. They evolved in a time when world attention was focused on Polish underground culture and people keenly awaited the next step of Grotowski away from what he saw as the restrictions of theatre. Such values as Grotowski promoted, that encouraged active rather than passive culture, seem anachronistic today in Poland. They belong to the particular consciousness of a certain period. Today people are being encouraged to start business initiatives, and activity in the arts revolves around raising funds, rationalisation of personnel and finances, and self-promotion rather than exploration.

Gardzienice's relationship to paratheatre — as Grotowski called his explorations — is ambiguous and not easily discerned, but it certainly had a formative influence on the company and Staniewski. The company members rarely discuss inspiration and sources and avoid comparisons. They would rather be deemed inspirational, creating new cultural trends not following them. Staniewski is evasive about his relationship with Grotowski. This he displays both in conversations and concretely in an interview with Richard Schechner: 'I don't like to speak about my connection with Grotowski. Ask Grot about it.'[1] In spite of these obstacles, the obscure paths which led to the creation of this rural theatre company can be clearly traced through the activities of student theatre and paratheatre.

The main path to follow to Gardzienice is Staniewski's, the Artistic Director and leading inspiration and energy of the Association. His story ends with a vivid description of falling off his motorbike in the village and then deciding to settle there, impressed by the land's geographical sweep. It begins with his first contact with professional theatre after graduating in Humanities from Cracow University. This was in three projects with Teatr STU [2] of Cracow in 1970 as an actor. Firstly an actors' workshop piece entitled *Landscapes*, secondly one entitled *The Wandering Master of Kosciej* by Ghelderode and most importantly, the landmark production of *Spadanie — Falling*.

STU grew quickly from being a student theatre group performing for local and mainly student audiences to a nationally and then internationally renowned full-time company. *Falling* was their third production and was based on, amongst other texts, the poem of the same name by Tadeusz Różewicz. *Falling* comprised elements from numerous poems, political speeches and philosophical writings and evolved with and responded to the politics of the time. It was 'a continual motion of marching, encircling and grouping.'[3] It had strong visual and physical elements, a documentary nature, a large ensemble of thirteen and a devised, flexible composition, all typical of student theatre groups.

One major element of STU's practice was their use of music, as this Polish critic's description indicated:

> *The role of music was in the foreground of STU's work... In STU they almost always sing their texts... music is part of the staging, it shapes the movement, creates not only the atmosphere... but is in competition with the word in establishing the dynamics of a performance.*[4]

This description could equally be applied to Gardzienice's work with their use of song to lead out the movement and to create the score of the performance. This might have had its roots in Staniewski's brief spell acting with them. In STU's theatre however, songs were used primarily to convey important concepts and texts for a political end, much as Brecht and Piscator used them. They became a means to underline and emphasise, whereas for Gardzienice the main function of song and music is to express emotion, create mood and dynamise movement — a notably different emphasis from STU's. Perhaps the use of music in STU's work shaped Staniewski's thinking, but this is impossible to quantify.

The theatre groups that were born in the late 1960s and early 1970s were not exclusively for people trained in theatre. Their multi-disciplinary nature was visible in their accessibility for a range of actors such as Staniewski, himself from an academic non-drama background. In the first half of the 1970s Grotowski began to take this open attitude to its limit through paratheatre. This was not to express political or social ideas but rather to promote fresh attitudes to culture through research into the nature of human expression. Its aim was to free participants from restrictions of text, acting and theatre form and to reinstate the value of collective action on a small scale.

Grotowski's laboratory-based work of the early 1960s had concentrated on the harshly disciplined training of a select group of performers. This led to public showings of their performances at international festivals which sent shock waves through the artistic world. They redefined the aims of theatre practitioners everywhere with their explorations and approach and the notion of 'poor theatre' — a theatre stripped of its superfluities to focus on the actor who is rigorously trained to maximise their potential; the actor's almost religious sacrifice to their craft through training and their openness or 'Gift' to the audience in performance; adjustments in the relationship between actor and audience that altered with every production. His methods, as described in *Towards a Poor Theatre*,[5] became a 'kind of new Bible for experimental theatre groups in the world'[6] according to Osiński, a Polish critic closely attached to Grotowski's work.

Grotowski could only follow his success and achievements by a radical change of direction:

> If he is to remain faithful to his principles then Grotowski cannot, after 'Apocalypsis Cum Figuris', produce anything that could possibly remain within the bounds of what is broadly understood as a theatre performance. A step beyond the experience contained in the 'Apocalypsis' signifies an ultimate departure from the theatre into the unknown which, if it still lies within the realm of art, will probably become an entirely new form of it.[7]

Grotowski therefore moved into his 'post-theatre' phase. This new direction continued his earlier scenographical experiments in altering actor/audience relationships, eventually redefining the notions of 'actor' and 'spectator'. It was at the very start of these explorations that Grotowski first saw Staniewski in *Falling*.

Staniewski worked with Grotowski's company from October 1971 until May 1st 1976 when he left to continue to make theatre in a more traditional sense than the paratheatrical activities could allow. Paratheatre's parameters are mapped out in Leszek Kolankiewicz's retrospective, comprehensive analysis of the Laboratory's activities of 1970–1976, entitled *On the Road to Active Culture*. The basic premise was that anyone could participate in cultural activities as a maker/creator and not only as a passive recipient. It stemmed from a belief in the innate creativity of people and a fear that contemporary culture was open to large numbers but simply encouraged passivity. People read others' books, watch others' films and television programmes and a small number of actors in theatrical productions. Yet the audience cannot interchange with the actors within theatrical conventions and rigid boundaries remain. Burzyński noted how the Laboratory's last performance *Apocalypsis Cum Figuris* responded in the early 1970s to these new ways of thinking:

> What in Apocalypsis is theatre form, became more and more marginal and the degree of opening out the performance became so considerable that cases of spontaneous audience participation in the action began to happen; the majority of the audience, however, no matter how ready they were for it, felt the existence of a borderline which in the theatre divided . . . persons into active and passive participants.[8]

The frustrations of the restrictions of form led Grotowski on a path beyond theatre. Although this road would have its own disciplines, structures and laws, essentially it would not be theatre. The Greek word *para* means 'in relation to' or 'beyond'. Theatre comes from the Greek *theatron* — 'to see' — and as such implies an observer. In paratheatre an audience could not exist for there were only actors. Without this vital element of public witnesses, Grotowski began uncertain cultural explorations.

Grotowski's vision of paratheatre was not without its own controls. Creativity was encouraged not through vague, open structures but by strictly planned workshops and events led by the members of Grotowski's group and Grotowski himself. Theatrical forms were replaced by more flexible, evolutionary workshop ones. These were open to a large group of people from all over the world who were carefully selected. Numbers were restricted for the sake of practicality and to encourage activities in small as well as larger groups. People were chosen who either wanted or professed a need for the experiences that the company could perhaps provide.

Recruitment came partly through public announcements in newspapers and on the radio. People were asked to write to the company expressing what they might hope for and expect from engaging with them. After performances of *Apocalypsis,* those who were stimulated to seek further contact could stay behind to meet the group. In this way certain people were chosen to be public participants in the paratheatrical activities. There was no attempt to deny the elitism in such a process of choice. Just as Grotowski selected six new members to join his group from observing their practice, so they were searching for people with whom they felt common understanding and empathy. The need in paratheatre for close contact with others made this selection an important early stage.

Before wider public integration could happen, the foundations had to be laid practically and artistically, primarily to create a group with a common identity and aims. Whilst working in the Wroclaw theatre, a rural home for the group was also developed in a place called Brzezinka:

> The new group had installed itself in the forest after having found and purchased old buildings and a water mill. We had to renovate the whole place to make it usable. It was the first common meeting of the new group ... The movement into the forest (which is not a 'return to nature') helps to establish a rhythm of work different from life in the city, which is more inhibiting. It's the rhythm of space, time, freedom. And one is not haunted.[9]

Grotowski was not interested in creating a homogeneous theatrical commune in the mould of the Living Theatre but of giving the group fresh resources and a shared understanding of process. This base was vital not only for the purpose of providing a different geographical background to his research and a neutral starting point but also for cementing the group which contained several new members such as Staniewski.

In this initial closed period everyone was given time and space to achieve personal 'renovation', akin to the actual practical rejuvenation happening in Brzezinka. In relative isolation (there were brief occasions when they could return to their private lives), the focus was on both the individual and the collective, removed from any demands created by the presence of the audience or public. There was also an extensive alteration of the Laboratory's personnel structure as Ludwik Flaszen, the Literary Director, has pointed out. It is not stated who he is, but this 'advanced' man was possibly Staniewski:

> *The new young ones in 1970–1971 were given full rights from the beginning. Amongst the rest of us, the previous hierarchy was destroyed and everybody had to begin anew ... A young unknown man ... was now equal to Cieslak or Rena. As it turned out, he was leading the more important experiences. He was the most advanced of us all.*[10]

Grotowski kept overall artistic control but each company member could direct their own project as they wished, according to thier specialisation. The foundations were laid for the first public participation in June 1973.

The paratheatrical events and activities subdivided into numerous sections, shaped by the personal interests of a project leader and the size of the group. They took place in several countries, including America, Italy, and Australia and their first stage lasted for three years, culminating in 'The Mountain Project'. A wide range of physical, vocal and experiential work took place as well as more academic and performance-based meetings. The largest of these was the University of Research of the Theatre of Nations in Wrocław in summer 1975, attended by up to 5,000 people and including celebrated guests like Joseph Chaikin and Peter Brook. There are numerous descriptions of the 'encounters' that took place over these years, expressing with difficulty the simple and often repetitive actions that they involved. Many of the events used natural 'scenic' elements such as grain, water and honey, natural concepts such as the 'Beehive', which was a swarm of various activities, and isolated but distinctive countryside locations.

To define it succinctly, Grotowski's aim was to find meeting points between strangers and through creative harmony push others to expressive and emotional limits. There was an emphasis on sustaining effort over long periods of time in order to open the body and mind, and to reach beyond cliche to spontaneity, when thought immediately becomes action. As with Grotowski's earlier actor training it was a 'via negativa',[11] a process of stripping away masks to show something simple, uncluttered and unaffected. Action rather than observation was fundamental. Workshops were closely controlled and motivated by the group leaders to avoid them dissipating into effortless, rambling improvisation. Participation was demanding and for some encouraged falsity rather than honesty, with its own codes and sublimated expectations.[12] Yet with few imposed external objectives, self-motivation in the work was vital, otherwise it could lead easily to passivity or overindulgence. Contrived expression could come from forcing creativity rather than letting the form and contact with others draw it out of you. The prime objective of the leaders was to prevent such falsity and pressures. Most reports are positive poetical descriptions, acknowledging psychological and physical therapeutic values. Before looking more closely at Staniewski's particular role during those five years, these words of Grotowski on paratheatre might help to clarify his intentions:

> *Some words are dead, even though we are still using them. There are some that are dead, not because they ought to be substituted by others, but because what they mean has died. This is so for many of us, at least. Among such words are: show, performance, theatre, spectator etc. But what is necessary? What is alive? Adventure and meeting: not just anyone; but that what we want to happen to us would happen, and then, that it would also happen to others among us. For this, what do we need? First of all, a place and our own kind; and then that our kind, whom we do not know, should come too. So what matters is that, in this, first I should not be alone, then — we should not be alone. But what does our kind mean? They are those who breathe the same air and — one might say share our senses. What is possible together? Holiday.*[13]

The fact that the Polish word for holiday, *święto*, has more religious connotations than the English word (holiday can also mean holy day), adds a gloss to his statement.

There is scarce documented information about Staniewski's own projects, contribution and official role during this period. He worked alongside Grotowski as collaborator as he travelled extensively, involved in general organisation, recruiting participants and practical work. In the autumn of 1975, after the Wroclaw University of Research, Staniewski took responsibility for an exchange of work between experimental Italian theatre groups and the Laboratory, entitled 'General Stage — Island Experiment'. This was on a small island called San Giacomo in Palude and was in conjunction with showings of *Apocalypsis* and paratheatrical activities. In *On the Road to Active Culture* there is a participant's description of a workshop led by Staniewski. Although it is often unclear and embarrassingly personal, it contains some illuminating elements:

> *The sound moved me. I found myself running, on my bad leg. Włodek stopped the others from following me . . . The sound of my breathing and my feet gave me a rhythm . . . I felt the breathing of the 100 people in the centre. I transcended personal pain . . . I wanted to celebrate . . . Candles on the floor . . . Włodek's work was very real . . . there was an amazing sincerity and commitment in him that made me dizzy . . . I left Wroclaw quieted, not talking much. I saw more, listened for sound, noticed when people talked out of nervousness and fear, when they babbled, and also noticed those impulses in me . . . I had more of a need to be broken.*[14]

The tone of this account is reminiscent of a religious experience and brings to mind the trance dances of the Balinese, where self-inflicted pain is not felt because of the intensity of the experience. The trance seems to be induced through similar means as it would be in Bali: fire, rhythm and breath. This description reveals the long term effects of such an engagement that seems to continue beyond the form and time structure of the activity. It also has brought out a desire for psychological reconstruction in the participant. Unfortunately there are not more accounts of Staniewski's workshops available with which to balance this one. The only other written material is Leszek Kolankiewicz's description of the theme of a workshop that took place in Poland in 1975, and in Italy in early 1976 after the Venice Biennale:

> *'Meeting' conducted by Włodzimierz Staniewski, with the attention focused on the problem of contact, aimed at self-exploration and exploration of another person in the course of intensive common action, where a kind of improvisation almost smoothly turned, for instance, into concrete cultivation of land. Actions between people in enclosed space, though not limited by the walls of a building — a real island in the sea.*[15]

This account suggests little in particular about Staniewski's preoccupations or way of directing a project that is not contained within the wider remit of the paratheatrical events. It is interesting to note, though, the connection between theatre and everyday work, which would become a feature of Gardzienice's experiments, and the emphasis on islands or places distant from the centre.

From this cursory insight into Staniewski's interests and his relationship with Grotowski, it is possible to note experiences, objectives and concepts that shaped Gardzienice. Above all, these experiments intended to break down the assumption that actors are trained, exceptional individuals. In Gardzienice's rural meetings villagers can almost become creative performers, usually through song, dance and music. The paratheatrical experiments were not limited by human abilities. Similarly Gardzienice's terrain was far removed from the closed walls of theatres. Nature provided the scenography, sources of energy and revitalisation, and a home that lay outside theatrical connotations. In 1979 Staniewski defined 'space' in terms of Gardzienice's explorations:

> *I do not mean yet another 'closed circle' fortified by dry rules, rituals. I do not mean another stage. By space I mean an area and the substance of the land and the substance of the sky, bound by that area.*[16]

He was firmly wishing to redefine the rules of theatrical play and its playground. This meant that the villages and meadows could become a 'Theatre Space' as much as designated buildings.

Equally influential on Staniewski was the diversity of experience with Grotowski and the scale of events. They happened throughout the world with mass active participation and cultural programmes beyond performances and workshops alone. They involved public debate and research and wider communication of results and experiences was essential. There is much dense writing from this period, executed by participants who were occasionally journalists ('observers' were not allowed to simply watch but had to partake and therefore write from the inside), the project leaders and Grotowski himself. This was no idle experimentation but a carefully analysed and programmed progressive sequence of events. Within these there might be great freedom for the individual but structurally they were as precise as Grotowski's previous actor training. There were strict practical conditions that were always observed and minute preparation of environments in order to scientifically observe people at play.[17]

Much of Gardzienice's method of training can be recognised in descriptions of the Laboratory's practice. Continuous, often repetitive and very simple movements would provide a foundation just as Gardzienice use rhythmical ways of walking as a common motif. This might be spinning, walking or running — in and outside — often for long periods. Outdoors there were exercises in mud, water, the forest and the elements, and these would become important 'actors' in the scenario. Indoors, great care would be taken to create a very particular environment and atmosphere. Lighting would usually be soft and natural, using candles and blackout, and spaces were simple and clean, thus focusing attention on the actors and their action. This was a form of scenic design that was made to harmonise the people and space being used. As with 'poor theatre', decor was kept to a minimum. Some rooms also had to be both work and living spaces, perhaps for up to a few days at a time. They needed to be easily convertible into a sleeping and cooking area as some workshops placed an emphasis on participants simply living rather than playing together, and general communal activity rather than creative exercises. Such attitudes to space, including work in natural environments, are central to Gardzienice's practice.

Exploring the potential and range of the voice was also a key intention of several workshops. Movements were found that released songs and sounds, and through these emotional or imaginative responses. People were encouraged to let rhythm, their bodies and their imagination lead them, often into a trance or a heightened state. In this way they could lose the censoring control of logic, fear and self-consciousness. Seriousness was excepted of all participants alongside exhausting concentration and a perpetual state of readiness.

The work always prioritised group creativity and support just as Gardzienice always look for 'mutuality' in their training. This was at the core of Grotowski's research. The offering from the actor to the audience, the gift of the open mind and body, perfected in Ryszard Cieslak's 'total act',[18] pivoted in paratheatre on a shared contact between two participants. Grotowski:

> *There is a point at which one discovers that it is possible to reduce oneself to the man as he is; not to his mask, not to the role he plays, not to his game, not to his evasions, not to his image of himself, not to his clothing — only to himself. This reduction to the essential man is possible only in relation to an existence other than himself.*[19]

Participation might stem from personal motives but it should peak in an almost religious offering to the partner or the rest of the group. Only then will the process and its purpose be revealed in all clarity, allowing exploration of this debatable notion of 'essential man'. Gardzienice's meetings with villagers had a similar function of revealing to the actors the truth of themselves, as Staniewski describes it.

Broadly paratheatre changed theatrical perspectives and challenged definitions but altered little in practice. Today the term is rarely used and few practise paratheatre as a cultural activity. The premise of theatre without an audience means that it is not strictly theatre. The public were never allowed to observe paratheatre which would have been tedious. It dealt with internal processes and had no intention to be communicative or visually stimulating. Its highly personal and closed nature has meant its effects have remained limited but it has partly become submerged into more specific kinds of drama work, such as psychodrama and drama therapy. It redefined the nature of cultural activity, just as Solidarity did on a social level, but the craft of acting was not extensively explored beyond Grotowski's earlier research. Paratheatre has perhaps had some influence in opening the boundaries of theatrical space, yet it is almost impossible to say how it has specifically influenced theatre groups — in their choice to lead workshops, perform on the streets or engage with a new audience, to name three possible examples. In spite of its temporary influence it could be said that it was at the forefront of cultural explorations in the 1970s.

Gardzienice reflect the combination of Grotowski's two main periods of activity, of performances and paratheatre. By being a cultural organisation rather than a producing group of drama workers they are open to all types of paratheatrical activities. Their practice involves performing and rehearsing, but they regularly organise training workshops, festivals and symposia and lead their own fieldwork. They encourage people to actively reengage with their own perhaps dormant culture and become performers, extending the notion of 'actor' to its limit.

Gardzienice's practice shares other hallmarks with paratheatre: encouragement of physical and vocal participation; a reluctance to allow observation of their work; seriousness and dedication; use of rural environments to work and live in and a flexible spontaneous work schedule — they often rehearse through the night and plan progress day by day. Yet Staniewski's relationship to paratheatre was ultimately ambivalent, with his desire to make theatre and his difficult choice to leave Grotowski in 1976 — to abandon the rather academic research in order to explore a simpler path among the people of Poland:

> *At the climax of Grotowski's paratheatrical work, I left his laboratory to do very profane theatre. I started with Rabelais' 'Gargantua and Pantagruel'. I showed this work to people in the villages because I was embarrassed to show it in the larger towns. This work was absolutely on the other side of the wall from Grotowski's Lab ... As soon as I left the Lab in 1976, I wanted passionately to make a theatrical performance. The people working in the Lab's 'holiday' phase were very disgusted with me — 'Oh he's the one in the movement who is betraying it for theatre.' For me it was very important to make something with its own performative architecture, possessing more than changing ceremonies and rituals.[20]*

Staniewski's participation in paratheatre heightened his understanding of how to encourage creativity and push people to artistic extremes. Yet his decision to return to a more pragmatic path shows a rejection of paratheatre as an exclusive activity with no relationship to an audience.

Staniewski's connection with Grotowski should be followed to its end. Although the former wanted to return to more formal theatre structures, his fieldwork and search among the rural people for 'native culture' proved surprisingly close to Grotowski's continuing research. From 1977–1980, when Gardzienice were most intensively leading fieldwork, Grotowski and a multinational group from various disciplines travelled to various parts of the world to research what Grotowski called 'source techniques'. This was not as direct subject matter for a performance as was the case for Staniewski but to discover and observe the primary roots of culture. One result of this journey was that Grotowski formed a new collection of people where each member came from a particular cultural background with different experiences, practice and expectations. In this 'Theatre of Sources', as Grotowski labelled it, he was searching for mutually comprehensible actions and gestures, addressing the debatable notion that there might exist a physical universal language. While Staniewski was travelling to the people to learn directly from them, Grotowski was selecting certain individuals with a strong sense of their native culture to continue his refined research.

Apart from his world-wide wanderings to seek out new practitioners, many of Grotowski's activities took place in Poland, revealing a close connection between his and Staniewski's preoccupations. Kumiega described one development in the Laboratory's plans from autumn 1978:

> *The decision was also made at this point to extend the theatre's new policy of taking their participatory work to other communities within Poland. In the late autumn there*

was a tour to the small Polish town of Tarnobrzeg — again with presentations of Czuwania *[vigil], and participatory workshops directed by the actors.*[21]

In August of the same year, Gardzienice also worked in villages in the Tarnobrzeg area. Grotowski's group activity in *Czuwania* involved sustained movement in a natural environment and was workshop-based, possibly with young people from the area. It was a very different contact with the community from Gardzienice's meetings with old people and presentation of elements of performance. Yet it is interesting to note how their paths crossed so closely, after Staniewski had supposedly 'betrayed the movement' by his departure from the laboratory and his return to theatre-making. Kumiega's use of terminology like 'presentations' also undermines the significance of Staniewski's betrayal.

The two directors are still in contact with each other and in 1991 Tomasz Rodowicz, Musical Director of Gardzienice, went to Pontedera in Italy to observe activities related to Grotowski's research into the nature of ritual. There he is working closely with song, using folk songs and discovering their potential in the actor through simple movement. This is with young performers. The paths of these two directors will continue to cross, with Staniewski being inexplicit about his relationship with his 'master' and Grotowski's influence on him.

The enduring influence of Grotowski and paratheatre is evident in Gardzienice's personnel which has kept a core from its earliest days. In 1977 Staniewski was invited by Lublin's Society of Theatrical Culture to initiate workshops in the village of Gardzienice. For this he used collaborators from Lublin theatre group *Scena 6* (with whom he had been working after leaving Grotowski) and elsewhere. Most important among these were Henryk Andruszko and Rodowicz. The latter still works full time with the company as actor, Musical Director and flute player. Andruszko is still active with the company as collaborator and actor in *Avvakum* but he does not perform in *Carmina Burana*.

The other senior members of Gardzienice graduated from Higher Education in the 1970s and, like Staniewski, none of them specialised in drama. Their backgrounds are varied, but they were all influenced by Grotowski's activities. The vast growth of student theatre groups and the accessibility of paratheatre made 'actor' training at a drama school for three years seem unnecessary for people not wanting to enter the main repertory theatres, for which formal training was obligatory. Student and experimental groups were not looking primarily for talent or skills but an aptitude for making theatre, and a personality that would fit into their particular way of creativity and life. Many groups like Gardzienice therefore provided their own training as part of the working process. Theodore Shank has described the situation in American companies during the 1960s and 1970s, which I believe is comparable with Poland at the same time and which is still true of less mainstream groups:

> *Often out of necessity, the companies provided theatre training because the participants had none and because the objectives, techniques, and styles of the new work required skills which were not taught in the universities nor practised in the older theatres.*[22]

For some companies, who were developing their practical methodologies and who were perhaps influenced by Grotowski's 'via negativa' in their acting style, traditional training might even be seen as an obstacle when recruiting. Acting schools often have their own house style which is passed on to students. Experimental companies in Poland preferred to work with actors who could learn and adapt.

In 1978 and 1979 more members joined Gardzienice, including Mariusz Gołaj, Jadwiga Rodowicz, Krzysztof Czyżewski and Anna Zubrzycka-Gołaj. All were previously non-professionally involved in theatre. Czyżewski stayed until the end of 1983 when he left to develop his own work, in particular the use of poetry in performance. He then founded Teatr Arka and later *Fundacja Pograniczne* (The Across-Borders Foundation). This company of which he is the Artistic Director, is based in the north-east of Poland in a palace which they bought in 1990 and are restoring. Their work and policies are similar to Gardzienice's. Czyżewski refers to Gardzienice as his initial inspiration and creates no illusions that what he is doing is unique or has no forebears, for with them he received his training. Jadwiga Rodowicz left her role as a full-time actress in 1990 to pursue university teaching and her specialist study of Japanese culture.

It can thus be seen that the core members of Gardzienice were involved in the formation and activity of the company over a long time period, developing from and challenging the concerns of paratheatre. In 1993 the Association had the full-time members of Staniewski, Tomasz Rodowicz and Gołaj (who leads the physical work and training) with Zubrzycka-Gołaj as a senior member. Dorota Porowska joined in 1986 and became a senior member, but she is too young to have been involved in paratheatre. The same is true of Catherine Corrigan from Britain — she has been working full-time as a performer since the autumn of 1990 — and of Marianna Sadowska from the Ukraine, who joined the company in 1992 as performer and Choir Leader in *Carmina Burana*. The core company has changed slowly, yet the specific influence of paratheatre has faded as the surrounding circle of personnel has changed.

1992 was a year of further change in the group. A core performer, Grzegorz Bral, left the company in December. Stanisław Kral, a former school friend of Staniewski's, also departed at a similar time. He has been administrator and technical manager for several years. He left to set up his own business and to spend time with his family in distant Wroclaw. In 1993 it became evident that Zubrzycka-Gołaj would leave the the company during 1994. Pressures on company members vary with each individual, though several seemed then to be frustrated and frequently exhausted, and some were seeking temporary project-based work elsewhere, in part to help make ends meet financially.

Gardzienice's work and daily patterns often seem to have the fluid nature of paratheatrical workshops, though with objectivity one can see how most events are tightly manipulated and controlled as the Laboratory's workshops also were. They have successfully balanced private, developmental, almost 'laboratory' work with public performances, meetings and workshops. Yet will it continue to be financially feasible, for example, to conduct the 'in house' training which Gardzienice once offered new company members? The commercial constraints on Polish theatre today mean that labour intensive and long workshops for small numbers of up to twenty people, or work akin to paratheatrical explorations cannot easily be justified. The economic regulation which Western models of funding demand, in terms of rationalising expenses, do not co-exist comfortably next to Gardzienice's open structures. An era seems to have drawn to a close: a period which began with the protests and student expression of the 1960s and 1970s and which led to the openness of paratheatre, which gave a broader theoretical base for theatre. The roots of Gardzienice grew in a distant time of self-trained, marginal groups, shaped by paratheatre. Now different attitudes to culture and money are being established, which threaten to undermine these traditions.

5

TRAINING

Gardzienice's performance style is rooted in a concrete training method. From their beginning the group extensively used vocal and physical exercises. This training is one aspect of their activities which has been unaffected by social and political changes. It has remained consistently exploratory and stimulating and has not lost contact with its initial inspiration from Bakhtin. This is partly because of its flexibility, as Staniewski has suggested:

> Training with us is an open matter; there is no method in the sense of an applied normative system. I don't ascribe systematic categories to our work process. But we do use certain sets of exercises which probably have a completely different character than those proposed elsewhere . . . Training, as I understand it, is necessarily a mutuality of two live presences. It is sharing energy, warmth. As if love-wrestling.[1]

Their training grew from the experience of the collaborators themselves, initially inspired by Grotowski and paratheatre. The absence of formulae or categorisation has allowed regeneration and the influx of new inspiration and has prevented the training from becoming a closed system. Their training evolved gradually in response to the creation of each of Gardzienice's performances. It began with theories of carnival, inspired by Polish native culture.

Gardzienice's training has many dimensions which need to be distinguished: it is central to the making of performances and thus involves the fabrication of images, the exploration of texts and the building of a repertoire of acrobatic and physical movements to name just three examples; it may stimulate the gathering of material from rural contacts (gestures, songs, texts, stories, superstitions), which are then incorporated into it; it continually expands the company's repertoire of folk songs and music with which to make contact with people in Gatherings and Expeditions; it hopes to create a fit ensemble prepared for the rugged fieldwork; and it is to adhere to and encourage a specific aesthetic as well as a way of working and living. Performers were gradually formed who were spontaneous, creative and musically and physically extremely able. Through such specific demands their training became unique. It has the distinctive stamp of Expeditions, Gatherings and the previous experience of the participants, (particularly Staniewski's contact with Grotowski), imprinted on it.

As the company evolved and expanded and led public workshops, their acquired knowledge had to be transmitted. Outsiders were introduced to the company through practical investigation into the group's already existing processes. By this means, others gained insight into Gardzienice's way of making theatre and could thereby increase their own training vocabulary. The group itself were enriched by such contacts which stimulated and clarified their own work. An accumulation of skills was not important in the workshops but rather an atmosphere of security and trust was built where participants could explore artistic techniques and self-expression according to Gardzienice's approach. The small scale and limited participation in the training have meant that it has developed only at the group's pace, led solely by their own discoveries and the material of each performance.

Minimal theorising has surrounded Gardzienice's training for it is best explained by practice. There is almost nothing written about either its development or its role within their practice. It tends to include active involvement for all, be they observer or actor, with analysis not encouraged. This absence of material is attributable to several causes: limited access to a usually hermetic world; the difficulty of finding a language to describe movement and vocal exploration; and the need to analyse a very slow, personal process. It is also easier for critics to assess public aspects of theatre, such as policy and performance, when daily existence and working methods can be inaccessible or too demanding in terms of time commitment. Mariusz Gołaj has written briefly about Gardzienice's training[2] from his earliest participation to his present role as leading instructor. This document gives valuable insight, but it is understandably extremely personal. Most of my analysis is therefore based on my own participation in and observation of workshops and Gardzienice's own more closed training. I have separated the body and voice which is anathema to their approach yet which makes this material more accessible. The section on voice and music precedes that on the body because in Gardzienice's creative process, physical action is built from a musical base.

Voice, Music and Sounds

Gardzienice's vocal training has three basic elements: an inseparable connection to physical movement and the breath; a non-technical approach (it does not refer specifically to physiological phenomena); and the use of folk songs from many cultures. This last area will be dealt with more in the chapter on interculturalism, the focus here being on more technical rather than conceptual issues.

In a workshop, Gardzienice usually teach several songs (mostly from their performances) to the participants or encourage them to sing their own traditional ones. In the former case, the words may be written down but the melodies are learnt through repetition and imitation. Tape-recorders are not allowed and the written music is never available for scrutiny. This can be considered a continuation of traditions familiar in oral cultures, where a song can spread like an infectious disease. It is reminiscent of the way Gardzienice collect songs in villages, though then they do occasionally use tape-recorders, but always discreetly and as a back-up resource after attempting to learn the song in the moment it is sung.

Folk tunes provide a base from which the training develops. These have usually already been transformed by Gardzienice so that they differ extensively from their original form. This evolution and elaboration might have come about from brief improvisations, which are described as 'ornamentations'. During the Latin song 'Ecce Torpet Probitas' from the Carmina Burana collection, the main ornamentation happens on the last word — *recedunt*. This might have become a fixed element in the song in the performance, yet it also stands as a training exercise. In a workshop this idea may be explored, as individuals are encouraged to briefly allow their voice to float and meander melodically above the drone that the others hold. Other such exercises involve the participants in copying the Gardzienice performers' lead. They must hold a dissonant chord within a song, for example, or follow a declining scale on the word 'Gloria', in relation to a partner's simultaneous slide. Such exercises are never subordinated to the actual task of singing the song in its entirety. A careful balance between the whole and details is always maintained. After the momentary ornamentation, the songs are sung in full, until the next person is asked to improvise around a word such as *recedunt*.

These exercises are technical, encouraging purity and accuracy of note, close listening and a sense of harmony. However, they are not technical in being physiologically related to the organs of the voice or resonators, as many teachers would approach vocal work. I have never heard words such as larynx, soft palate or projection in the rehearsal space or during workshops, though I have heard approximations — the actors might be asked to root the sound lower in the body, in the diaphragm. Gardzienice prioritise group singing rather than voice-work on individuals' specific problems. For Gardzienice, song warms up the voice, but it is as important for what Gardzienice call 'mutuality/*wzajemność*' — a close, physical interaction. Staniewski has said that 'Song as a line of life of the voice is a leading element in the performance. Singing not only warms up the voice, but creates a harmony in the group, a common vibration'.[3] Only once that is achieved are the finer performative effects of music considered. Staniewski's words are not those of someone who is primarily concerned with the specific technical details of voice-work, but someone who is looking for larger achievements. Gardzienice do not instigate 'voice warm-ups' as a separate unit in training, as is familiar in many British acting schools, but sing as a part of the total creative process. Perhaps Staniewski's contact with village singers — who are not overtly conscious of the performance-related aspects of their music and their audience, but sing for themselves — has allowed him to think in a simple and refreshingly broad manner about the possibilities of song in theatre and in actor training.

The connection of the voice to action is part of Gardzienice's continual search. Porowska has often been praised by Staniewski for her constant movement to lower her centre of gravity and place a song or sound within her body. Sounds can be shaken out of the body, can echo movement, punctuate it and respond to it. In the 1991 workshop with Royal Shakespeare Company actors in Stratford, individuals ran up a wall and backflipped down with assistance from other participants. On landing there was an explosion of song from those supporting the acrobatic movement, the chorus. The choir must 'sing the action and performers' as Staniewski describes it. Practically this means that they must watch the movement and vocally inspire it, both rhythmically and in shades of tone. A connection between sound and action is of prime importance, be it within one body or in a larger network of people. The actor must be active with the whole of their organism and potential.

The vocal and musical score defines the physical shape of a performance. Songs lead out the action and provide a verbal text. However, the use of songs tends towards a rhythmical and tonal structure rather than a narrative sequence. Musical sections are slowly built up in rehearsal: songs might be connected through musical linking passages or only a part of them might be used.[4] They then might underscore a written text or accompany an action. Music provides the base from which all action unfolds.

The empathy between voice and body depends on breath for song rides on the breath and breath enables movement. One of Gardzienice's ways of walking (see Plate 1 (a) and (b)) is defined by a regular rhythm of inhalation and expiration, which leads the body and its steps. The same is true of the night-running, as will be explained in the section on the body. From a constant rhythm, ornamentations and improvisations can grow. Artaud's analysis of the actor's breath in the chapter 'An Affective Athleticism'[5] in *The Theatre and its Double* has many meeting points with Gardzienice's use of the breath. They both link emotion to breath, rooting expression and emotion by physical rather than psychological means. If someone is physically or vocally lost or floundering, breathing provides a base as the simplest of activities. Breath is thus the performer's key, encouraging emotional exploration and responsiveness or a neutral foundation, allowing exertion or tranquility.

All sounds can be used and words do not have a primary role. Vocal experiment is encouraged through exercises such as a basic one that is reminiscent of the gypsy vocal technique of 'rolling' — an improvisatory vocal, wordless duet. Actors make sounds to accompany Rodowicz's flute-playing, which comprises breathed noises rather than notes. The instrument shrieks and whistles and the voice must respond in a question and answer structure. Two pigeons coo in a bird's dialogue. Likewise, words can appear in many guises. Latin words are chanted at treble speed so that the mouth is exercised by enunciating consonants and vowels. The phrase 'Ave formosissima', for example, is repeated again and again at varying rhythms, before it then breaks into the gentle song from which the words are taken and which carries that title. Words might be spoken but they are as valuable for their musical quality as their meaning. Along with animal sounds and laughter they make up the colourful lyrical weave of Gardzienice's perform- ances and training. Similarly company members use a broad range of acoustic instruments from many countries. Most of the group are proficient in one or two instruments. Musical accompaniment to training can also be the specific respon- sibility of collaborators such as the members of Kwartet Jorgi who provided incidental music for the Autumn 1992 workshop in Derry. In the earliest stages experiment is encouraged with little regard for auditors. Release and expression come before questions about quality, although these soon influence the process.

This openness of potential material could lead to confusion and chaos. The 'incantations — tweeting, whining and yells of the natural languages — in the spectacles of Brook's and Grotowski's imitators'[6] of Jan Kott's description, are avoided in Gardzienice's work by discipline and melody. Sounds are not com- pletely arbitrary but are controlled by Gołaj's precisely set physical and rhythmical limitations, Rodowicz's more intuitive judgements and Staniewski's energy and clarity of thought. 'Musicality' — as Gardzienice call a sense of musical and rhyth- mical harmony and understanding — is vital, be it in movement or the voice, but it cannot be forced out of people. To find it one can apply few rules but must listen to oneself and to others and keep searching by physical attempt. Gardzienice wish to encourage the freedom of releasing the restrictions of individual inhibi- tion through the dynamics of group singing. Yet rhythms and sounds are discovered only through the controlling devices of attentiveness and respect for collective rather than individual acts of creation. Solo flights can only take off from a firm choral base. Gardzienice's activity is based on a group identity and the power of the choral voice. It is driven by a search for the simplest instinct to sing together which perhaps exists in us all.

Flexibility of technique also comes from the songs Gardzienice choose to work with, which tend to dictate the practice. The three vocal parts of 'Ave formosissima' are sung on quiet, long sustained notes, which are difficult harmo- nies. This song therefore has its own 'training'. The songs that Gardzienice use, in many different languages and sometimes without words, set their own demands and have their own needs. The mouth must cope with Yiddish, Greek and Latin languages, to name but three. The body also needs to listen and respond to the rhythmic dynamics of the corresponding cultures, as reflected in their music. The light dance rhythm of Jewish music may be followed in Gardzienice's training —

as it may in their performances — by the sonorous chords of Georgian songs. In their vocal training, Gardzienice traverse the world. The broad range of songs denotes a comprehensive mixture of movements and styles of singing. Slavic folk songs have their own specific quality of lamentation, as all folk songs have particular qualities, chord structures and rhythms. A diverse yet highly specialised approach is specific to Gardzienice's vocal training.

For Gardzienice, music conveys important emotional moods and is linked inseparably to atmosphere. A workshop or rehearsal in the candle-lit wooden spaces of Gardzienice's workrooms relies on an ambience created through carefully controlled environments. The voice responds to this sensitivity. In the darkness it can soar to uninhibited heights. The electric lights do not need to be turned on to tackle a musical difficulty through the eyes and head when the ears and the body are used. Gardzienice reinstate the value of song by carefully preparing the conditions under which it can be released. As such, they recognise the importance of singing as a basic form of human expression. Such needs cannot be forced out of individuals but can grow more readily in carefully prepared circumstances, as Gardzienice continually prove in their vocal and musical training. Correspondingly, music is used to create atmosphere. Musicians play during meal-times, at workshops or during massages after strenuous exercise. This is a strong constant in their work and provides a base to all their activities. From this base the training can begin, action can evolve and eventually a performance be created.

The Body

A central and unique element of Gardzienice's training is night-running. Evening work usually begins with this activity, which might last anything from half an hour to an hour. In winter there is less running due to climatic constraints. Night-running for Staniewski has a particularly important place in their training. In unpublished conversations with me he has described it as 'the first word', 'a basic state of human nature' and 'initiatory purification before work'. Its conception possibly comes from Staniewski following the path of Artaud to the remote Sierra Madre Occidental region of Mexico and the Peyote-imbibing Tarahumara Indians. Like Artaud, Staniewski was struck by the magical beauty of the deep canyons and like many before and after them, by the energy and physical prowess of the Indians. Artaud was looking for "organic culture, a culture based on the mind in relationship to the organs",[7] away from civilisation, amongst a people in close touch with their environment and bodies. Nowhere was this more exemplified than in their running. For Artaud the journey had, above all, immense spiritual significance: for Staniewski too, though he took from it something quite tangible.

The Tarahumara Indians are renowned for running long distances, often 200 miles over two or three days in the rocky, difficult terrain. They run both for practical reasons — carrying messages, hunting — and for more competitive ritualistic ones, as demonstrated in races or *rarajipari*. Running is a well established tradition for the tribe and begins in early childhood. They do not run fast but show astonishing endurance abilities, never out of breath after long runs. 'Probably not since the days of the ancient Spartans has a people achieved such a high state of physical conditioning'.[8] One can see the obvious attraction in this for Staniewski: in their corporeal and mental ability, the sympathy between them and their natural surroundings personified in activity, and the combined practical and spiritual functions of their running imbued as a tradition. All these elements were adopted and adapted for Gardzienice's own night-running.

For Gołaj, 'Night-running has its own poetics, its techniques, which can be practised, its space which can be fulfilled differently each time.'[9] It liberates him, making him aware of others, 'naturalising' him both by heightening his consciousness of nature — 'the pulse of the earth and shooting stars'[10] — and that of natural human gestures and behaviour — 'breathing, the next exercise, mutuality, the group. Without any psychological consequences'.[11] In the darkness, the eyes lose their power and other senses control the activity. The body is warmed, muscles loosened and the mind prepared, almost cleansed of distracting thoughts. This is done in relation to a specific environment: in Gardzienice along the paths and sandy forest tracks or in Wales along cliff-top roads. In Stratford in 1991 there was only one evening of night-running which was at the actors' behest. Until this request, the idea was avoided by Gardzienice — I construed that this was due to the urban, populated environment. When the natural surroundings are too severely controlled by man, the necessary conditions cannot be fulfilled. Street-lamps then guide you and not instinct. Even in Gardzienice a car may occasionally disrupt the night-runners who sit quietly till it passes.

It is of value to explain the quality and purpose of night-running in detail for within it are contained most elements of training. It is also the first point of contact many people have with Gardzienice's training. Within the slow, rhythmical breath-driven stepping of the tight-knit crowd, there can be pauses for other exercises, not always proposed only by the leader. They might include acrobatic exercises such as cartwheels and backflips on the grass, or trust games (as they might be called), like falling from a high bank into waiting arms. As the group advances, the movement is never regular — the breathing may develop in a moment's brief improvisation and this structure may be echoed physically. Two people might break away to run downhill at a faster pace before returning to the shuffling crowd. A partner perhaps supports the other's head, so they can gaze into the star-studded sky whilst moving. Words are not used, but occasionally part of a song might grow from the breathing. There are no verbal explanations or observers, for the only participation possible is active. In spite of the pressure this creates, a safe environment is always ensured. The pace is slow, (it is not a jogging rhythm), so one feels able to run all night. On returning to the rehearsal room, however, one is aware of the energy and effort committed. Moreover, one feels the heightened consciousness bought on by the activity and deep breathing in the dark night air. The run is usually followed by a vigorous massage to further shake out and ease tensions in the body.

Night-running can be equated with the pre-liminal phase of a rite of passage, to utilise Van Gennep's[12] analysis of the three stages of initiation rites and develop Staniewski's description of its function. It removes the participant from the everyday, encouraging an altered consciousness and preparing those involved for the rest of the night's work. Night-running always takes place towards the end of dusk, as day is consumed by night. The human journey and distancing process is simplified by the natural passage of day into night.

Van Gennep's observations can be related further to the daily practice of Gardzienice, be it their own work or their training of others. If the rehearsal or work-session is viewed as the liminal phase, then there can be seen to be a post-liminal phase which allows for reintegration onto the everyday level. Schechner has described this phase as 'cool-down'. It might include anything from a meal to a conversation, but serves the role of 'restoring'[13] the performers as he puts it. In Gardzienice this is either shared food or tea after work, usually in relative quiet after the physical and vocal excesses of the previous session. In 1989 after performances of *Avvakum* in Gardzienice, the actors returned to the dressing-room to sit in silence and darkness for five minutes. Such as emphasis on transitions and preparatory processes gives value to each stage of the activity and defines each area. Acclimatisation phases heighten the capability of participants, as well as separating and thereby sanctifying the central core of activity. Night-running has both a distancing and a preparatory function, always located within a specific natural environment.

Staniewski always used to initiate night-running until after some time (no specific date is given in Gołaj's article) Gołaj was given the leadership. Now Staniewski participates occasionally. This transference of authority reveals how gradually the new members took increased responsibilities. Gołaj has recalled how his didactic role began most definitely when introducing the German performer Ulrich Hardt into a role in their second performance *Sorcery*. He describes the objectivity that integrating someone from a different cultural and theatrical context brought to the training. It took months for Hardt to sound the Polish texts correctly. Ways of moving, acrobatic techniques and the resources used for finding energy in moments of exhaustion had to be clearly transmittable to others. They could not belong solely to a private, inaccessible world. As well as discovering specific personal responsibilities in training, the company opened up through such encounters, becoming more self-conscious of their art in their need to communicate and practically define it. What for them was initially a means to create performances, transformed into a series of techniques and an approach that could be transmitted to others. It became a model process which could be both defined and shared.

Some theories for training perhaps arose from literary sources but they were soon submerged into the practice. Physical elements were taken directly from Bakhtin. His descriptions of the 'grotesque' body (see page 68) and laughter that undermines authority were concrete enough for the company to physically interpret them. Staniewski has worked closely with Zubrzycka-Gołaj to develop the art of the belly laugh. He turned laughter into a musical, rhythmical aesthetic form, that demands strict diaphragm control and physical looseness in allowing the body and the organs of the voice to release the sound. In such a way, theoretical ideas became exercises and through osmosis a theatrical device. The actors who created *Avvakum* studied icons under Staniewski's direction, which then shaped their movement and gestures, particularly in relation to positions of the spine. Staniewski has described the villages as their 'university', but one where observations are realised physically and not just intellectually. Bakhtin's theories were not only words on a page but surrounded them in a concrete form. With regards to *Avvakum*, Staniewski has written:

> *Although we've constructed a theatrical event of Bosch-like images, these could be replaced by pictures of the everyday work of the villagers. But to show the villagers at work would not be theatrical.*[14]

Bakhtin's writing on Rabelais provided a connection between literature and the environment in which Staniewski was operating. Such a process leads to a state that Bartok eventually found: 'Folk music became such a part of his thinking that even he didn't know when he was using elements of it.'[15]

Another theoretical notion found in Bakhtin's account of carnival that physically shaped the group's training is that of high and low culture. The tension between these two levels is central to Gardzienice's practice and is inherent in their actual contact with villagers, in the collision of two worlds of experience. It also exists in the villagers themselves, with their labour on the land and their religious aspirations. In Gardzienice's training and as a natural consequence of this in their performances, there is a corporeal relationship between earth and heaven. Their exercises include movements which root the body to the ground — low centres of gravity, wide-legged stances, stamping that pushes the feet into the floor. Alternatively there are ones which look towards the sky — explosive leaps in the air with the chest and stomach bared to the ceiling and upward stretches (see Plate 4 (c) and (d)). One exercise which bridges the two realms, is to reach up on tip-toes with an inbreath to then expire and collapse flat on the ground (see Plate 2 (a)). From one perspective this can be viewed as a simple stretch-and-release exercise, yet for Gardzienice it specifically relates to the dual worlds of heaven and earth. This dialectic is perceptible in many exercises, gestures and postures of their work and gives it a particular contradictory and dynamic energy.

These oppositional poles and the transition between them is reflected practically in a notion that is central to Gardzienice's training. This is the division of action into moments of 'strength and non-strength' as Staniewski describes it:

> *Human nature is built on two positions — one of strength from the earth up to the waist, and, two, of nonpower, from the waist up, which is always a kind of bowing.*[16]

Strength means that the body is rooted to the earth; it is charged with energy; it can provide a base for a partner to work with; it is simple, direct and firm. Non-strength is soft and delicate without excess energy; it can be easily lifted or manipulated; it can fly and fall or climb on another person; it is relaxed and open. An exercise that contains both elements is the rise-and-fall one, cited in the previous paragraph. Staniewski says that there can be a contradiction within one person in any moment, which can be perceived in what is almost a test exercise (see Plate 2 (b) and (c)): someone stands, their legs strong and the top half of the body bent forward, floppy and relaxed, with the head hanging down. With assistance from others, another performer climbs onto the standing person's back, one foot on the base of the spine and the other prodding and testing the shoulders and head and the extent of their relaxation. In this way the body is seen to be split in half, in two physical states. Any upward movement then returns to the ground or to the level of Bakhtin's 'material bodily lower stratum'.[17]

In their performances, the characters that Gardzienice create are allegorical, archetypal or choral. The training encourages exploration of human physicality and its representation within a cultural context, rather than psycho-physical or situation-based behaviour. The emphasis is continually on movement without psychological motivation. Cultural patterns of activity may be examined and exploited. The bowing of Russian Orthodox worship, which suggests humility, was used in the creation of *Avvakum*. Gardzienice's physical exploration thus reflects Bakhtin's own analysis of physicality, which is linked inseparably to social and cultural circumstances. One clear influence of his writing on Gardzienice's physical training is seen in their interpretation of his description of the 'Grotesque Image of the Body'.[18] In this chapter he elaborates on Rabelais' redefinition of the body:

> *The stress is laid on those parts of the body that are open to the outside world . . . apertures or convexities . . . , ramifications or offshoots . . . the open mouth, the genital organs, the breasts, the phallus, the potbelly, the nose.*[19]

Rabelais' world-view is defined from this physical perspective. One example of this is the open mouth, which swallows and consumes, is equated with hell, the underworld, and in a typical inversion the anus. This is not to say that Gardzienice merely accentuate these parts of the body in a farcical style, for their connection to such ideas is much more subtle and integrated. They are not revealed so much in phallic horseplay but in such moments in *Avvakum* and *Carmina Burana* as when an actress shyly opens her bodice to reveal her breasts. Similarly the mouth is always open in training and performance for singing.

It is important to reiterate that Gardzienice do not literally interpret Bakhtin's writings. What his influence means for their training is an emphasis on physical exertion and excess, finding artistic value in 'grotesque' shapes and a reinterpretation of the body. Accentuated breathing from the open mouth is one typical example of this. Likewise, all movements should be led by the spine or the pelvis. They consider the latter as a centre for movement and a source of energy and are disinterested in the fussy, smaller expressivity of the hands and face. It is difficult to say whether such traits in their exercises were directly inspired by Rabelais in Bakhtin's vision or assimilated[20] by more complex routes. The interaction between Gardzienice's idea of 'assistance' and Bakhtin's market place collective underlines this two-way and complex traffic of ideas.

'Assistance' (*asekuracja* in Polish) has a vital role in Gardzienice's training. This is not simply an idea that encourages responsibility for safety when trying difficult acrobatic manouevres, nor is it just a means to ensure heightened physical and spatial awareness of each other. Both these factors are important for creating an ensemble, yet as Gołaj notes, 'Gardzienice's training — "moving" (*poruszanie*) as we call it — was never just for the sake of a theatrical effect, or for the creation of champion superstars. It was, it is, for practising mutuality (*wzajemność*).'[21] What Gołaj is highlighting is how their exercises can possess a more complex purpose than is outwardly immediately visible. The principles that underlie the exercises have value over and above the exercises themselves. Yet he is also saying how their work relates to people as social beings in encouraging direct, unguarded communication between them. Assisting one another is central to this.

This almost therapeutic function reflects the concerns of Grotowski's paratheatrical activities, which prioritised the subjective effects of creativity rather than its objective presentational values. Gołaj seems to possess similar concerns. Detailed work on the person can have artistic results, but that is not the primary demand or starting point. Simple human actions and relationships are of the essence. With this perspective, the concept of assistance relates to Bakhtin and the crowd that moves as one with collective intention:

> *This festive organisation of the crowd must first of all be concrete and sensual. Even the pressing throng, the physical contact of bodies, acquires a certain meaning. The individual feels that he is an indissoluble part of the collectivity, a member of the people's mass body.*[22]

In Gardzienice's training of other groups, one sees this throng of arms and bodies — people not isolated by differing thought processes and egos, but united by sequences of exercises. In their workshops Gardzienice continually demand of the participants physical support and care. As well as a specific function related to physical training this liberates people from everyday social patterns and restrictions as they become part of a mass organism with its own rules and rhythms. The work has a therapeutic function in psychological and experiential terms: 'It gives to its members an experience of larger human physicality, where individual self-consciousness sharply diminishes'.[23] The value for the participant stems from this looser relationship between conscious thought and movement. If viewed from the outside this movement can be given theatrical form and an aesthetic content.

There are three basic training exercises that are described by Staniewski as 'mutuality exercises' (see Plate 3). They involve a pair engaging closely to take each other's weight, demanding a flexible arch in the back of the one being manipulated: firstly one lays their partner down across their knees as they squat; secondly they make their partner lean backwards to lie on the floor supporting them by their head: thirdly they let them lean backwards, facing them and supporting them hand-to-hand. All three demand that the partner being manipulated has a relaxed top half of the body and strong legs, but most of all they demand a transference of attention from the head to the pelvis. This area must lead the movements, with the head relaxed and inactive. Many find this adjustment very difficult and the top half of the body is stiff with the head tensed, wishing to initiate the moves. The ability to control and release is important for attaining a sense of mutuality, trust and agreement, when the timing should be coordinated, the breathing together and the position balanced (see Plate 4 (a) and (b)). Often a key for this understanding and control depends on the spine, which is a vital element in all Gardzienice's work, as Staniewski has revealed:

> *Certain exercises I consider ours. For example, the crossing of the meridians of your body with the meridians of another. In Polish folk culture, the spine is called the 'cross' . . . the meridian is exactly where my cross fits his (her) cross. When we speak about the cross, it is not the training that's important, but rather the cultural way of using the cross.*[24]

Once togetherness is achieved, one can improvise and add movements and more strenuous acrobatic balances become easier (see Plates 5 and 6). Exploration must stem from a base of mutuality.

Even these mutuality exercises could be related to Bakhtin's physical emphasis in that he continually refers to non-cognitive simple actions such as defecating, eating, and urinating. Whatever the connections, it is more important to return to tangible issues and note the end point of Bakhtin's analysis, which always confirms the positive and regenerative nature of Rabelais' imagery. Lower bodily functions lead to rebirth, such as Pantagruel's floods of urine which become life-giving springs or human excrement which becomes a fertiliser. Carnivalesque images are ultimately rejuvenating. Gardzienice's training is liberating, creative and continually challenges both its own process and other methods. It thus remembers its origins in the celebratory influence of Bakhtin, which so directly inspired Gardzienice's first performance *Spektakl Wieczorny/Evening Spectacle*, as the next chapter reveals. The open contact in workshops, which encourages both give and take, helps Gardzienice continually seek new direction. Gardzienice's training never promotes stagnation or stasis and rarely encourages passivity. It is fundamentally regenerative reflecting the most positive attributes of the carnivalesque.

The training is remarkable for its specific relation to Gardzienice's performances. Staniewski has said how each creation has its own training attached to it. Hasidic spinning is peculiar to *Sorcery* (see Plate 7), bird-like walking and mutuality exercises relate to *Carmina Burana*. This notion can be elaborated by noting how their workshops take the participants through a similar condensed process that the Gardzienice members have been through in creating their performances. When a workshop takes place in Gardzienice village, it is closely akin to the company's daily working methods, with night work a priority unless administratively implausible.

Workshops offer participants a combination of experience and education, of activity and observation. Often workshops include demonstrations; participants then try the sequence shown or an element of it themselves. One instrumental factor in encouraging attempt and understanding of the mechanics of exercise sequences is Gardzienice's notion of 'intentional training'. To some extent this is called 'marking through' in Britain, denoting a lightly sketched attempt rather than one with full effort. Positions of hands and the body, points of contact and the rhythm are practised in a safe context, before the actual movement is tried with total body weight and physical engagement. Yet even to achieve precision and mutuality 'intentionally' is a demanding exercise in itself. Depending on the ability of the group and the demands of some sequences or acrobatic exercises, 'intentional' work is extremely difficult in itself, yet it can help build confidence slowly.

When Gardzienice demonstrate exercises, workshop participants are encouraged to find an active role in supporting the presentation, which might be repeated several times. They ostensibly become a chorus, responding to the protagonists. By following the performers' paths and stepping so fully inside the creative process, participants can learn a great deal about Gardzienice's work, without theoretical explanation or analysis. Reciprocally, Gardzienice can develop ideas and find new material which may later be included in performance or test already extant sequences. This is usually constructive for both parties. For Gardzienice, training is an integral, creative part of their working process and is not viewed in isolation from their other activities. For them it offers a chance to gather new material for a performance as much as a Gathering may do.

However distinct Gardzienice's training seems, it is not a closed method and any such description would be firmly rejected by Staniewski. Theories have been distilled through years of practice and are conveyed to students physically, usually by imitation. This has created unwritten principles and codes, such as minimal talking during or after work. Constant, sustained effort is another, with actors encouraged to continually move and not lapse into a passive observational role when there is a demonstration. If there is a big hiatus, accumulated energy can dissipate, for which everyone must take responsibility. There is a seriousness expected of all attending the workshop, a temporary commitment to its values. However, Gardzienice members will help lighten the atmosphere if there is too much tension, as they did during their workshop with Royal Shakespeare Company actors in 1991. The unspoken dialogue between the participants and the leaders is greatly enhanced by the size of the Polish ensemble, as the difficult and very different experience of teaching Gardzienice's exercises on my own has shown me. In Stratford there were seven trainers for thirteen actors, an excellent and rare teaching ratio. In Wales in 1989, there were nine for some twenty. By this large presence, attitudes, principles and techniques are passed on subconsciously and through imitation. A Gardzienice workshop can be magical and overwhelming.

If words are used they either introduce and perhaps verbally set rules, or explain a radical development or readjustment. In Stratford in 1992, Staniewski introduced the company with a warning to the actors not to look for instant results, but 'to do' before asking questions. He chose the metaphor of a fisherman, uncertain of what they will get but bound to catch something. In Wales in 1989, words were necessary under Tomasz Rodowicz's direction, to explain that the workshop was finishing early and to suggest that we leave the place rather than stay simply because it was convenient. This change came because the company felt the work had reached a natural conclusion after a climactic evening spent singing in a cave. Words have a function which usually relates to the larger aspects of training, the whole structure and methodology, rather than to the teaching of individual etudes.

Since my first contact with the company in Wales in 1989 I have taken an active role in many workshops, in Italy and Gardzienice with groups ranging from Polish Higher Education students of mixed courses to a group of professional British performers. They have varied from two weeks to three hours, as in

Italy. Usually the training is for people interested in theatre and Gardzienice's work. In Italy it was simply for people who stayed behind after a performance. A group of Polish students who study, amongst other subjects, Social Anthropology and Polish Literature, attended brief workshops in Gardzienice three times a year from 1990. An interest in drama is not a prerequisite; again reminiscent of Grotowski's multi-disciplinary paratheatre participants. Gardzienice occasionally provide more specific training for people to work alongside them in their rehearsals for an open time period, as several British people have done. What such variety demonstrates is a lack of formulae; each workshop will take its own direction according to the environment, its length, the participants and the broader stage of development of Gardzienice's own work. Most contacts come from people who have seen a performance or through an administrative mediator familiar with their work. Advertisements are rarely used to attract participants.

The training programme for Royal Shakespeare Company actors which took place in 1991 and 1992 has raised the profile of this aspect of the company's practice. Thirteen actors were carefully selected for the 1991 four-day session, which had to fit into their heavy performing schedules. Staniewski found the actors to be very tired at the beginning of the workshop and used the training partly to build their energy. This first workshop was part of a wider programme of actor training at the Stratford base, but in 1992 Gardzienice were invited specifically to develop the previous year's collaboration with a new group for two weeks. This also included a brief overnight sojourn in rural Yorkshire with night-running and evening training work. Unfortunately both workshops remain only briefly documented with the second one completely closed to outsiders. The 1991 workshop was closed to observers, though I watched one day's work and there was a final demonstration for an invited internal audience. I also had informal discussions with participants. Albert Hunt wrote an article about the demonstration 'The Staniewski Method Comes To Stratford' for The Guardian (7.1.92.) and The Stage and Television Today (9.1.92) included a more thorough one of mine 'Polishing Up On Classical Theatre' — (see Appendix for an edited transcript). The collaboration has hardly been publicised in Britain whereas in Poland it has been mentioned in many sources. It seems likely that the process will continue to develop, for both parties speak highly positively about the slowly evolving programme.

There is little distinction in both structure and content between external training for outsiders like the Royal Shakespeare Company actors and the internal company training. The former is a microcosm of the latter. The main differences are the more personal intensity in Staniewski's training of his actors and the lack of separation between training and rehearsal. The process of devising a performance is closely linked to the notion of letting the performers acquire new abilities and continually demanding more of them, so that they are disciplined and expand their range through an essentially creative process. By looking for the '*trud*' or obstacle in an exercise and overcoming it, one will improve. Through demands and questioning, one develops. Before all activities there are meetings for precise preparation, not necessarily involving the whole company, and afterwards there are rigorous note sessions led by Staniewski, who is always meticulously detailed.

It is not easy to objectify the relationships between the newer performers and the trainers, particularly Staniewski and to a lesser extent Gołaj (Gołaj's role is more simply that of a teacher rather than an Oriental-style 'master', as Staniewski's role often seems). They vary radically from individual to individual and are of course highly personal. There are some common features: the demand for discipline, the encouragement of continual self-exploration, an intimate relationship with Staniewski that is subordinate and respectful even when he is aggressive and undermining, and a need and desire to propose ideas and take responsibility for the process and results. Actors are expected to be continually self-motivated and develop work alone, outside of rehearsal time with Staniewski. There are no union restrictions in Gardzienice and the actors work in a way at which many British actors might baulk.

There is little room for laziness, tiredness, or complaint in the process. If Staniewski wishes to work briefly and individually with one performer, the others will be sent out, even into cold night air, until his intention is achieved. The British director Katie Mitchell has described some of these seemingly negative practices which eventually yield rich rewards, with reference to a full-time Swedish actress who worked in Gardzienice in 1989 and 1990:

> Helen started to cry: 'If you are going to cry, then cry,' Włodek said. 'You are acting crying, don't act'. He paces around the room . . . They try the same duo harmony again and again, the others singing quietly a background harmony in an attempt to buoy up Helen's and Jacquie's song. Helen shouts at Włodek. Włodek shouts back. You can hear the tears in her voice. Haltingly, falteringly, she continues. Again and again. Then suddenly her voice erupts out of her — strong, clear, deep . . . He had used a very aggressive, attacking energy to open Helen, knowing that the only way to prize someone open is to break them — take them past the tear barrier.[25]

Such a description of course raises many questions about the role of a director, their privileges and their right to manipulate performers. One should not judge Staniewski's approach by this one incident. Yet however aggressive or painful the process may be, Staniewski's approach is part of a deep search which relates directly to the actor's processes. He is provocative, forcing the performer to plunge emotional depths and attempting to cut through psychological and physical resistance. He is not interested in cliches but gestures, actions and movements which perhaps surface from the subconscious or from depths which may even surprise the performer. He demands submissiveness of his actors so that they are malleable. His criticism of Helen and instruction to her not to act, precisely pinpointed her particular acting problem of self-consciousness and a tendency towards demonstration. She left the company after a year and a half for many reasons, not least her inability to both accept such forceful direction and form a mutually respectful relationship with Staniewski. After experiencing what was for her a magical workshop and being desperate to work with the ensemble, she found that in the long term, in the daily reality, the contract was not for her. It is a fine balance that only a few non-Poles can tolerate, with the heightened difficulty of an alien social context and language. Yet the rewards of this training can be many.

Analysis of how Staniewski works with his actors helps to explain the precise intentions of Gardzienice's training. The actors need to be flexible and tough, both physically and emotionally. Staniewski expects them to open up a range of possibilities, to be receptive to his suggestions and those of other performers and to have stamina. The process must become instinctive in them so that they can achieve a level of ease which Staniewski often indicates by the Gnostic poem: 'I sing and I am sung: I dance and am danced'. They must work closely with each other, listening and sharing, yet be forceful enough to make propositions and individually develop them. These creative suggestions are always put into practice and eventually comprise the performance, though at any stage they can be rejected by Staniewski. The actors read literature on the subject engaged with and suggest textual contributions. For *Carmina Burana* reading included several versions of the 'Tristan and Isolde' story and related myths and tales, amongst other less obvious materials. To a large extent there seems to be a collaborative process as one might expect during such a long period of creativity. A typical rehearsal might involve the actors meeting in the evening to be joined later by Staniewski. By the time of his arrival they may possibly have a solution to a problem from the night before, may have learnt a new song or may have a proposition developed. Yet the idea that it is a collaboration is strongly negated by the fact that Staniewski ultimately controls all elements, particularly in the later stages of rehearsal when his direction is more dominant.

The actors must also be prepared to be flexible in their commitments outside work, for a rehearsal session will last as long as it needs to. Holidays are taken when they fit into Staniewski's plans for the group. Organisation is Staniewski's domain, and the actors have learnt not to ask what work they will be involved in, either in the short or long term. Besides, much can change very quickly in the rural environment and in Poland's unstable economic climate. This uncertainty can put enormous strain on all members of the company which ultimately may lead to a lack of motivation or negative feelings of powerlessness.

This problem of the balance between a personal life and the company life is exacerbated by the fact that Gardzienice rehearse and train at night. Both of the previously married couples have had, and in one instance still have, school-going children living with them in the village whose timetables are not flexible. These may clash with the fluid rhythm of Gardzienice's patterns, ultimately exhausting those who individually have to operate within two frameworks. The priority placed on rehearsals and training always gives their work admirable seriousness, but pays scant regard to social and other needs that exist outside the practice. The restrictive times for social engagement can be a pressure which inevitably builds up with time. On an Expedition, Staniewski described to Pawluczuk one function of exhaustion for his ensemble:

> *It's not that you've got to be tired. But physical effort is necessary in order to become more resistant psychologically, to develop a real sense of togetherness, to prepare you for what is to come.*[26]

This is perhaps valid for short periods but as a permanent state can create severe personal problems and tensions within the group.

There is a similar ethos apparent in their training. It is a cliche that breaking through the tiredness barrier can encourage thrilling developments in a creative process but this has been frequently evident in their work. The previous example cited of Staniewski training the Swedish actress Helen, related as much to her fatigue as to her resistance and acting problem. However, I have also witnessed many nights of staggering exhaustion and uncreativity. As they get older, the actors of course become physically more prone to tiredness after exertion. Staniewski sometimes forces and at other times abandons rehearsals. Occasionally it almost seems that he is disciplining the actors for the sake of it — as a reminder of his authority and their submissiveness and to stress the need for them to be prepared for and rested before work. Constant readiness and commitment and night-work are all idiosyncratic and well established traditions of Gardzienice's group culture. These are remarkable and yield rich rewards but the social implications for the individual can be disastrous. For the company members such problems are not even debatable. In their commitment to the group they offer themselves to that culture and those rules — the individual's will is thus sublimated to the higher artistic concerns of the company which is controlled by the director.

Much nurturing and development is achieved behind closed doors and is part of a specific relationship between Staniewski and the individual performer. Describing even a part of his relationship with Helen paints a misleading picture — a total perspective on a private process can scarcely be achieved. Such relations between performers and directors, and even between collaborators and a director are very flexible, responding to the demands of any moment. My own association with Staniewski, even though it is not specifically within the training structure, varies and continually surprises, though he is always demanding and rigorous.

Gardzienice's training still has a personal and specific nature. It is led by and linked to the core of collaborators and has not outgrown them. Those such as myself can only teach or pass on to others our own highly personalised response to it, an adaptation and understanding of principles rather than a method. Such individual interpretations bear little relation to the group's own approach, which has such potential enabled by the sheer number and range of talents of those leading the work. Their training is also personalised by the fact that it has evolved alongside their performances. Social and political changes and the international success of the group have therefore had minimal effects on it. Residential facilities in Gardzienice are now more regulated by the company and they can use their own larger spaces, yet this has made little substantial difference to the training itself, simply allowing it to take place on a slightly larger scale. It is rooted in the group's history, in their original theoretical inspiration and in the personal stories of the company members. It remains the strong distinct core of all their activities, at the heart of their Romantic quest to create a new performer, or at least a new being.

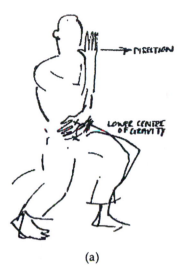

(a)

(b)

1. Ways of walking
(a) Walking with a low centre of gravity and with a gliding linear movement.
(b) Walking in the space with movement leading from the pelvis.

(a)

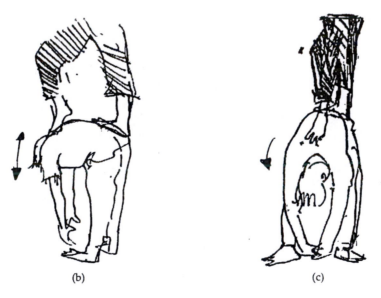

(b)　　　　　　　　　　　　　　　　　(c)

2. Strength and non-strength
(a) One stretches up and is then supported as they release to fall to the floor.
(b) & (c) One stands on the base of the other's spine, a position of strength. The upper torso must remain relaxed and is tested by the partner's prodding foot.

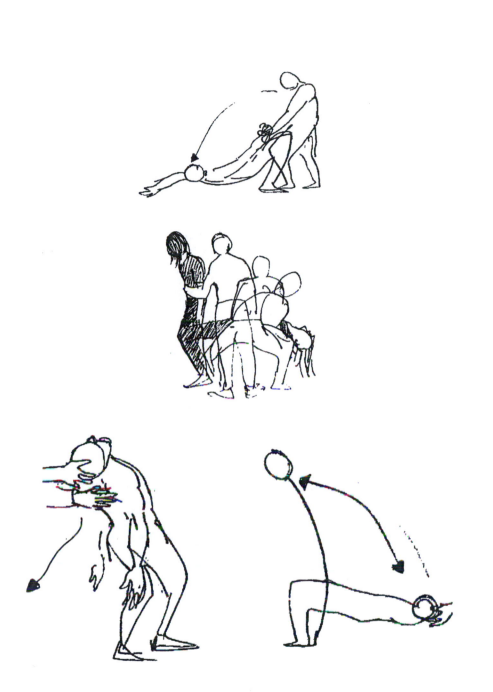

3. The three mutuality exercises

(a)

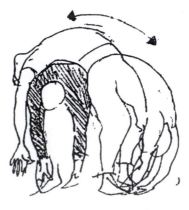

(b)

(c)

(d)

4. Warm-up exercises
(a) One person leans forward and back giving their weight to two others.
(b) One partner takes the other's weight across their back.
(c) & (d) Two people run towards each other, jump and bounce off each other's chests to land and hold each other in a crouch.

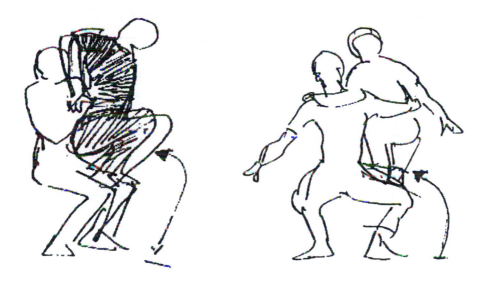

5. Basic pair balances

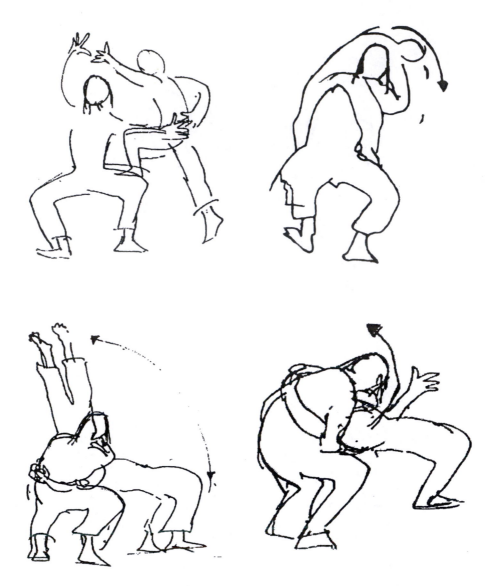

6. Acrobatic sequence
One partner stands on another's thighs, reaches over them to link their arms around
their waist and pivots over their base to the floor. The sequence can be reversed,
impulsing up from the floor.

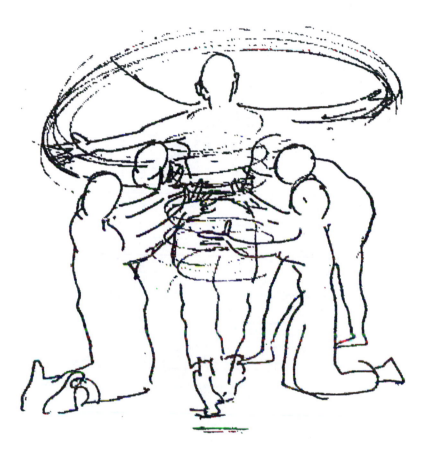

7. Hasidic spinning

8. The sign outside the company's office in Lublin. Photo: Paul Allain

9. Włodzimierz Staniewski, Artistic Director of Gardzienice. Photo: Hugo Glendinning

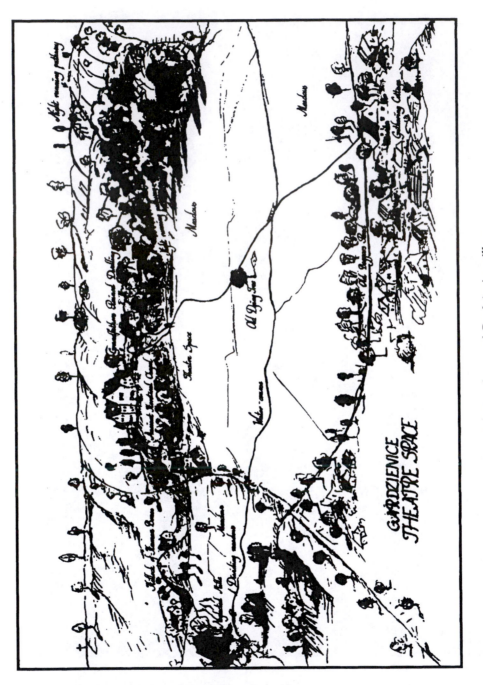

10. A fictional map of Gardzienice village.

11. The road into Gardzienice. Photo: Paul Allain

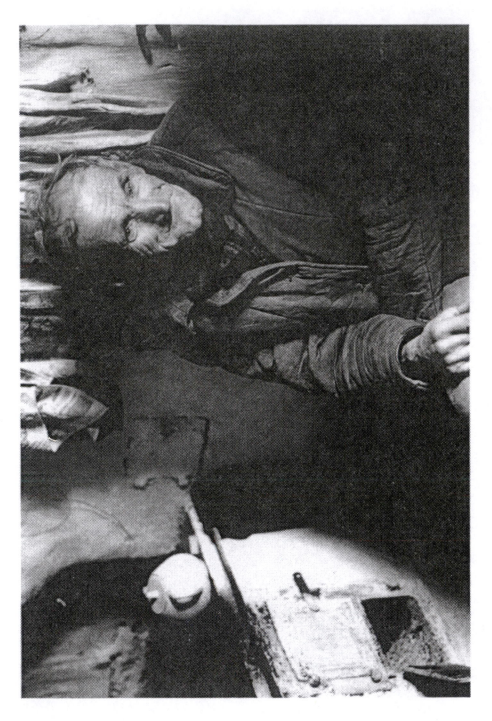

12. *Dziadek* in his home (1989). Photo: Hugo Glendinning

13. The Gathering Cottage in Gardzienice (winter 1990–91). Photo: Paul Allain

14. The wooden mill in Gardzienice (spring 1991). Photo: Paul Allain

15. The *oficyna* undergoing restoration (winter 1989–90). Photo: Paul Allain

16. The night-running path by day (winter 1989–90). Photo: Paul Allain

17. The set of *Avvakum* in St John the Divine Cathedral, New York.

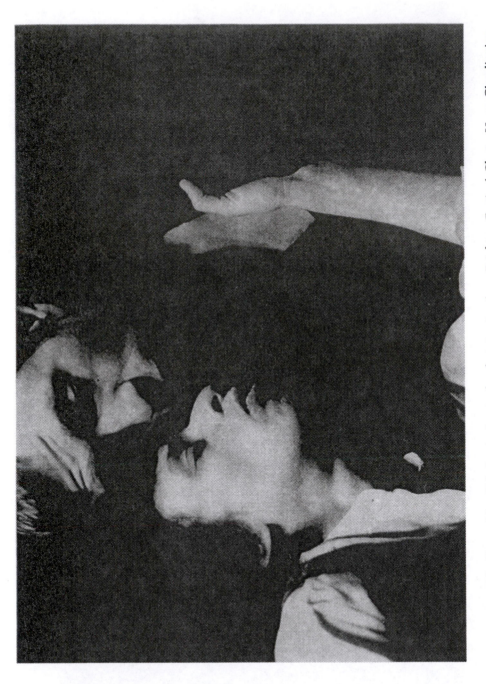

18. Suzanna Pilhoffer and Jan Tabaka singing in the choir in *Avvakum*, Brighton Festival. Photo: Hugo Glendinning

19. Grzegorz Bral being turned round on the wheel of torture in *Avvakum*.
Photo: Hugo Glendinning

20. Dorota Porowska in *Carmina Burana*.

21. An impromptu musical gathering in a tomato field in Priozornoie, Bessarabia, Ukraine (September 1993). Photo: Paul Allain

22. Villagers singing at home in Lisowe in the Ukraine on the border with White Russia (September 1993). Photo: Paul Allain

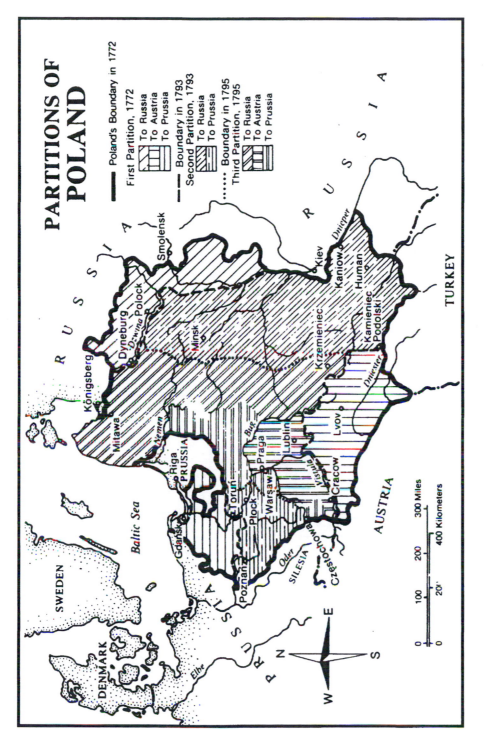

PARTITIONS OF POLAND

—— Poland's Boundary in 1772

First Partition, 1772
To Russia
To Austria
To Prussia

– – – Boundary in 1793
Second Partition, 1793
To Russia
To Prussia

······· Boundary in 1795
Third Partition, 1795
To Russia
To Austria
To Prussia

SWEDEN

DENMARK

Baltic Sea

R U S S I A

Smolensk

Königsberg

Dyneburg

Dwina Polock

Minsk

Riga

Mitawa

Niemen

PRUSSIA

Gdańsk

Toruń

Płock

Poznań

Warsaw

Praga

Bug

Lublin

Krzemieniec

Kamieniec
Podolski

Kaniow

Human

Kiev

Dniepr

R U S S I A

Dniester

Lvov

Vistula

Cracow

Częstochowa

SILESIA

Oder

Elbe

P R U S S I A

AUSTRIA

TURKEY

N
W   E
S

0   100   200   300 Miles

0   20'   400 Kilometers

23. A map of the Partitions.

6

PERFORMANCES

'Ethno-oratorio' is a term that was coined by Leszek Kolankiewicz to describe Gardzienice's performances. In the same essay he said that their work was capable of 'radically refreshing our image of musical theatre'.[1] This points to the heart of Gardzienice's explorations which have extended the parameters of theatre. Such new terminology can help define their output which seems minimal according to Western criteria — they have made four performances since 1977 which are all shorter than one hour. Yet as Kolankiewicz's search for descriptive terms indicates these are innovative and complex. Time spent on rehearsals is a priority for Staniewški, meticulous, obsessive perfectionist that he is. The company's idiosyncratic, intricate performances reflect this commitment and their dedication. Owing to the limited documentation of their productions other than simplistic reviews, most of my writing is a personal response rather than an assessment of others' analysis or descriptions. The only productions of Gardzienice's I have seen are *Avvakum* and *Carmina Burana* and these many times, so I will concentrate on them, after briefly considering *Evening Spectacle* and *Sorcery/Gusła*.

By tracing the development of their performances one can see the creation and evolution of a particular aesthetic. The pattern of this growth is most visible in their first three works which are closely connected to each other and rooted in Expeditions. The first two performances were almost prototypes for the third, *Avvakum* — the piece that established Gardzienice internationally as a group that could create a substantial work of high and individual quality. *Avvakum* could stand on its own without being contextualised by a Gathering or Expedition, though it was often performed with a Gathering or as part of an Expedition. The fieldwork was at the core of the creative process which built *Avvakum*, but it did not depend on them for its presentation. Extending this detachment from their rural work, Gardzienice's last piece *Carmina Burana* is almost divorced from Gatherings and Expeditions. Considering their performances in the context of their sources, their evolution and finally their presentation one can detect two phases which *Avvakum* bridges. The first phase refers more to carnival and village life and the second to literary sources and the international artistic circuit. The Romantic quest for rural inspiration and sources has been replaced by urban demands, and performance material has come increasingly from written rather than orally transmitted sources. By taking this overview it can be judged how far Gardzienice have travelled from their initial aesthetic and principles — how the low has become dominated by the high, to use Bakhtin's division.

Evening Spectacle and Sorcery

Gołaj[2] has described how there was already an established group of nine people, a practice and a methodology when he joined Gardzienice in 1979. The company had created and toured *Evening Spectacle* (inspired by Rabelais' *Gargantua and Pantagruel)* which had initiated the Association's activities in Gardzienice in 1977. They had been on several Expeditions in Polish villages and had begun to realise Staniewski's theoretical 'Rural Programme' that was then extended in his paper 'For a New Natural Environment for Theatre'. There was also an international and educational perspective from the beginning, with specialists and young people from around the world invited to participate for short periods in practical work or to join them on Expeditions.

   Evening Spectacle was last performed in 1986 and it now exists only in documentation: in articles and in a poor quality film recording made by the company. It would usually be performed as part of an Expedition as an offering from Gardzienice. It was framed by the arrival and disappearance of the cart which was used to transport belongings during an Expedition. It thus seemed to grow out of and return to the company's wanderings. Osiński has described the style of the piece and revealed its close connection to Bakhtin:

> The action is violent, aggressive, shocking... Never do the people remain indifferent... the show is held outdoors, as day fades into night... It is actually a series of short and long exercises in acting... this loose structure makes for great flexibility... the show is never the same twice... is marked by sharp counterparts, characterised by ambivalence, an interplay of opposite meanings... There is no story line or narrative.[3]

This description paints a vague picture, yet Osiński's response underlines one central prerequisite of the performance. It was to be a point of direct emotional and physical contact with an audience, rather than a presented example of the group's culture and artistic ideals to be judged from an analytical distance. It was energetic and loud as the village setting and crowds of noisy villagers demanded, and was open and responsive to each new environment and situation. *Evening Spectacle* reflected Bakhtin not only in its subject matter but also in its open structure, its exaggerated and provocative style and its 'market place' setting and audience. It was a total exposition of his theories, as indeed was an Expedition of which it formed a culminating part. As Osiński points out, it was closer to training than performance with no narrative, message or logical structure. It is in this stage of Gardzienice's existence that we can perceive their closest affinity to Bakhtin, theoretically but also practically.

The texts of this first performance were a mixture of Rabelais' story, parts of Mickiewicz's *Dziady*, an ancient Latin hymn to the Virgin Mary and an old English song. It also included some dialogue and speech collected in villages. The vocal score comprised an illogical sequence of texts, songs and sounds, contained within short episodes. A fixed structure was avoided, reflecting carnivalesque principles. The body was the dominant instrument of communication with the mouth always open in song. Filipowicz has described a performance that she witnessed in rural Poland in 1981. Her description reveals *Evening Spectacle's* carnivalesque techniques:

> The spectators stand in a semi-circle in front of burning torches surrounding the perfor-mance area. Several half-nude actors run in pulling a cart . . . Grabbing and waving the torches, the actors jump on and off the cart in acrobatic feats and humorous pantomimed etudes . . . Dancing orgiastically, the actresses bring in a huge straw figure — the zmij of Slavic folklore — and set its long, protruding phallus on fire . . . Occasionally the actors run into the crowd, hugging and kissing the peasant women amid shrieks of delight, wonder and excitement . . . The performance speaks more to the senses and emotions than to the intellect and reason. There is no storyline or psychological development, only a quick succession of brief and dynamic episodes. The organising factors are fast-paced rhythm and a dazzling interplay of opposites.[4]

By observing working movements, gestures of the body and vocal patterns in the countryside, Gardzienice reeducated themselves. By looking in the market places of Piaski and even Lublin they discovered the reality of Bakhtin's words: 'A spec-ial carnivalesque, market place style of expression was formed . . . market place speech and gesture, frank and free . . . liberating from norms of etiquette and decency'.[5] The textual material chosen began in the villages, evolved there and returned to them, transformed through the focusing lens of Gardzienice's artistic vision. They were actively realising Mickiewicz's quest to find inspiration for Slavic culture from rural sources.

Włodzimierz Pawluczuk, who has written extensively on Polish traditions, has described the various effects of this performance on a rural audience as he witnessed it in Polish and Italian villages at the end of the 1970s. The performances ranged from the cathartic to the antagonistic. He qualifies his observations by saying how Staniewski probably prefers a response which shows that the audi-ence have been provoked:

> When the atmosphere is intensely ludic, all 'obscenity', touching and provoking the aud-ience, enhance this state, they amuse, cause laughter; something like a carnival develops. But when the audience is, for some reason, tense, alert and tends to reflect, then every-thing that escalates the carnival may cause a transfer from Version 1 (Full acceptance) to Version 2 (Provocation) or 3 (Rejection).[6]

From the beginning Gardzienice were trying to create visceral, emotional theatre that would extract a reaction through the devices of shock, disruption and energy that in its turn solicits a response from those being met. Although they were aware of their origins in a higher cultural background, the performers eschewed any intellectualising which might distance the audience. This was theatre that could communicate to a particular people on a direct physical level and that would serve the function of finding a meeting point between native culture and Gardzienice's own urban and more analytical culture. Events were scarcely controlled and outcomes would vary widely. Usually, though, Gardzienice would measure *Evening Spectacle's* success by the extent to which it would provoke the villagers into activity. With provocation as a central aim of the performance, *Evening Spectacle* was presented throughout Europe and especially Poland, mostly in villages. It spoke to and was made for those who could answer it from their own native culture, and was thus rooted within a particular idiom and context. It had clear artistic intentions, a 'natural environment' (in terms of addressing a specific audience in a specific place which correlated to the content and form), and was spontaneous and open.

Sorcery was the next creation, premiered in May 1981. It continued to explore the idiom of folk culture but moved between two contexts — it was performed in festivals and cities in Europe and beyond, as well as in small rural communities. It extended Staniewski's interest in Mickiewicz, being based on Parts One, Two and Four of *Dziady*. This was within the tradition of avant-garde Polish theatre in its use of the classics, yet was rooted in the reality to which their fieldwork exposed them. As in *Evening Spectacle*, texts were not treated in their entirety for a narrative purpose and selections were instead used to create a collage of sound that had equal footing with action and song. The Polish critic Dziewulska has described how the lines were spoken in an incantatory fashion, a mixture of speech and song. This gives us an indication of Gardzienice's approach to the vocal transmission of texts. Filipowicz has described the performance in more detail:

> From Mickiewicz's drama, Staniewski has taken the central situation of the rite and a handful of spoken lines, including the peasants' incantations, the ghosts' confessions, and one of Guslaw's monologs (sic). These bits and pieces are intercut with additional Slavic folk materials, Christian imagery and elements of the Hasidic culture which was born in eighteenth-century Poland in the rural area around Lublin...the movement of Sorcery is carried largely through a tension between the sacrum and the profanum.[7]

Lines were fast and explosive, enunciated emphatically yet not always audibly, riding on long streams of breath — reminiscent of prayer in a Russian Orthodox service. These rhythmical speeches were broken by laments, for as Staniewski has often stated, the lament is the dominant tone of the Slavic people. The piece was driven by opposition and contrast.

Sorcery was more literary than *Evening Spectacle*, with greater emphasis in performance on its content. It again used disjointed episodes and the 'grotesque body' described by Bakhtin, with the men often just in trousers and employing exaggerated gestures, ways of moving and postures. It had fewer basic exercises and physical sequences and moved away from training towards theatre. This could be seen in the historical references, which made the performance more complex and referential than the rather expository *Evening Spectacle*. It echoed Grotowski's *Akropolis* with its allusions to the extermination of the Jews and in its use of a grotesque performance style:

> *The girl runs in in a frenzy, at first with an oven pipe, shouting 'Arbeit macht frei' three times; then she brandishes a pitchfork and utters the spell of the old peasant woman from the region of Lublin . . . The men appear once in the attire of peasants-cum-workers, at other times as a crowd of Jews in long black coats.*[8]

Sorcery was a transposition of Bakhtin's ideas into a theatrical forum, though as Fillipowicz noted in her article 'Expedition into Culture', it drew less directly on 'the popular-festive carnival spirit' than did the previous performance. This is primarily because it used more religious symbolism, be it Hasidic spinning (the predominant physical motif) or images of the *Pietà*.

Bakhtin's theories were still evident in the piece in numerous ways: the harsh juxtaposition of ideas (a priest makes love in a church and in the next moment becomes Jesus in the *Pietà*); the flexible barrier between audience and actors (the *soltys* or mayor of the village leads in the chorus who are temporarily dressed in shawls, boots and clothes, similar to those of the audience); the inversion of everyday rules (the priest is the ill-motivated sorcerer); the use of 'billingsgate' or market place language as it is more familiarly known. All these factors reveal the nature, style and conception of this twenty minute piece and its close relation to Bakhtin. It shows the extraordinary mixture of religious cultures, from Christian to pagan to Judaic, which permeate Gardzienice's work. This reflects both Bakhtin's interest in folk cultures as well as Poland's complex ethnic history. The performance crystallised village life and clearly grew from material gathered during Expeditions.

The effects of *Sorcery* on the audience were similar to those outlined by Pawluczuk with regards *Evening Spectacle*. It was intended to provoke, which could as easily result in a negative response of fear and rejection as much as it could open the people to share their own culture. Filipowicz describes one such failure in a village context in her first *TDR* article.[9] This was attributable to many causes too complex to recount here. Partly the performance played on the people's naivety and superstition to such an extent that it resulted in the collapse of the performance and the audience leaving. Yet the performance was just one small element in the whole activity of an Expedition. *Sorcery*'s success or failure in the villages depended on such factors as the contact made during the Expedition, the unity of the villagers and the careful preparation of the space. It by no means depended solely on the piece itself. Similarly, when presented at festivals, it was part of a programme that included other parts of Gardzienice's practice. This is described by Filipowicz in her second article in *TDR* about the group's visit to Baltimore in 1986.[10] *Sorcery* had an important function as a climax to a sequence of events and stood more comfortably as such than as a performance on its own. Yet the nature of festivals, with their more formal division between workshops and performances for example, inevitably affected *Sorcery*.

Filipowicz's later article reveals how much *Sorcery* was a loosely structured open performance that could alter radically. Elements of *Sorcery* were affected by *Avvakum*, as Filipowicz notes, observing that "the new darker version of *Sorcery* serves as a prelude, setting the tone for *Avvakum*".[11] Osiński has also noted how a quite different performance was presented at European festivals than that which had been shown in Polish villages.[12] A new group consciousness evolved, as their work began to be presented outside Polish villages and the company responded to this new context. The original mission of the group to make contact with Slavic native culture shifted to also accommodate the company's desire to share their experiences with international theatre audiences. The contradictions which exist in Osiński's following statement reflect the split in focus which began to appear in Gardzienice's activities:

> The *Sorcery* is, in principle, a part of the Expedition; it can also be a starting or crowning point, it can also appear mid-way. Especially in the cities, it is shown as an autonomous show which may, but does not necessarily have to transform into an encounter with people.[13]

At international festivals the spirit of carnival could not be recreated in short Gatherings with disparate urban audiences so unlike the tight-knit communities of rural Poland. *Sorcery* was critically well received, but in such contexts the extraordinary world of Expeditions and Gatherings was communicated primarily through the distancing media of slides and films. Gardzienice's theatre began to become subservient to representation and self-explanation, divorced from the rural reality and experience of Expeditions. *Sorcery* could then be viewed as an exotic artistic interpretation of European folk cultures, as Filipowicz's account of its uncomfortable reception in America showed. Urban Gatherings could only be a pale imitation of their rural counterparts. In spite of the difficulties of the framing context of their performances in urban conditions, the creative, regenerative tension between high and low culture was still visible in Gardzienice's next performance *Avvakum*.

Avvakum

Avvakum was made during Martial Law and has been called a Martial Law piece by Polish critics and even Staniewski. This added to its resonances as it toured the world. Premiered in August 1983 in a remote church in Italy, it has since been performed in venues as diverse as Saint John the Divine's Cathedral in New York for that city's 1988 Arts Festival, to a lake-side open air venue in Lappland and numerous villages throughout Europe. *Avvakum* was often accompanied by a Gathering, which on a simple level served the purpose of explaining its Russian Orthodox context. It has occasionally been performed on its own, lasting from thirty-five to forty-five minutes depending on its pace. Since 1991 it has usually been presented with *Carmina Burana* and without a Gathering. It has constantly evolved and developed as such a long life for a theatre piece might demand. New people have taken over from those who initially created the performance and the choir that vocally accompanies the action expands and contracts, even including myself for three performances in Gardzienice. The performance's tone has altered since 1989 when I first saw it. As the memory of Martial Law has faded in the light of post-1989 changes so has the performance become lighter and more humorous.

In spite of the flexibility of the number of people in its choir, *Avvakum* has a closed structure if compared to *Sorcery*. Its form is dictated by a rigid sequence of songs and tightly orchestrated movement sequences. The base of the perform-ance comes from the Russian autobiography (1672/1673) of Archpriest Avvakum. As a leader of the Old Believers, he was persecuted by government-backed Nikonian groups who wanted to reform the Orthodox church, under the guidance of Patriarch Nikon. The results of the conflict were violent as Filipowicz elucidates:

> For his stalwart defence of the old Russian Orthodoxy, Avvakum was declared a heretic and thrice deported with his wife and children to Siberia, where he spent some twenty-five years. A mighty spokesman of the Old Believers, the zealous, pugnacious Avvakum became an inspiring example of unflinching defiance no matter the risk or cost. The gov-ernment, unable to stop the spread of the Old Believer movement, ordered that Avvakum die on the pyre.[14]

His autobiography offers graphic accounts of his suffering, torn as he was between desire and holiness, and describes his battle against reforms. It is told with zeal and religious fervour, with tales of exorcisms that he led, his purifying self-flagel-lation and his long miraculous journeys through the empty Siberian landscape. It moves easily between superstition and brutal fact and is a vital piece of Russian historical literature and folklore.

The other main source for *Avvakum* is the Digression to Part Three of *Dziady*. This links in closely to the story of Avvakum's exile with its homage to Poland, descriptions of the enforced banishment of Polish youth and intellectuals to Siberia in the early part of the nineteenth century, and accounts of the building of St. Petersburg:

> *Through the snow into the wilderness*
> *Trundles a kibitka, like a wind in the desert*
> *Here the eye finds neither city, nor mountain . . .*
> *Never people wanted — but Tsar's whim and whose orders to build*
> *not city for people but a citadel for himself . . .*
> *Oh, poor man! A tear runs from my eye*
> *And my heart pounds when I consider your deeds*
> *I sorrow for you, a poor slave!*
> *Nation of poverty — sorrow your fate, the only one is your heroism great —*
> *Slavery!* [15]

The Digression is a crystallisation of the sentiments of the whole work. Gardzienice thematically integrate it with Avvakum's similar story of repression from more than two hundred years before. Anti-Russian sentiments are not straightforward or overt in the performance, but they become more evident if it is viewed in the light of Martial Law. The piece is not prescriptive and is as much about abuse and repression by individuals as well as organisations or nations. It is not a generalised nationalist critique or lament.

Programme notes for *Avvakum* divide the performance into thirteen segments of action. Each section has an equivalent song and occasionally songs. Some of these, such as 'The Stage of Exile' are repeated four times, though on each occasion with a different physical and musical accompaniment. The piece has an episodic and repetitive structure, reflecting and dramatising the Russian Orthodox service. Whoever has witnessed a service will recall the almost hypnotic state induced in the auditor by musical repetition. Often a service will last for two hours and comprise very few hymns, and elements of the music have immense theatrical potential. Gardzienice learnt the non-liturgical Russian Orthodox songs of *Avvakum* from the Lemko communities of Southern Poland. Not looking for logical continuity, they avoided the Old Believers' songs, perhaps broadening the resonance rather than limiting it by focusing only on the small community of Polish Old Believers. Staniewski took elements of the music and transformed and speeded them up for dramatic effect. The hymn *'Pamiluj mia Boze'* moves through a range of rhythms to create a lively score for one section dubbed 'On the Stage of Exile'. *Avvakum* explores the distinction between music for worship and music for theatre.

Beyond music, numerous elements of Russian Orthodox worship which had theatrical potential were used in *Avvakum*: the transformative lavish costume of the 'pope' (or priest, to cite the Catholic equivalent); his recitations, which take place behind a screen with two doors, through which he occasionally appears; and the illumination of candles by the worshippers before the *iconostasis* or screen of icons. For the religious scenes and pictures of tortured devotion such as that which opens the performance, Gardzienice attended Orthodox services on Expeditions, went to the pilgrimage site in Grabarka and studied Russian iconography and religious gestures. The performance adheres to the carnivalesque play of oppositions, with depictions of the baser aspects of Avvakum's character undercutting his religious nature. For the scenes of lust, drunkenness, violence and sacrilege, village life was observed on their journeys through rural Poland. The creative connection between performance and Expedition can be clearly perceived in *Avvakum*. Its Bakhtinian contrasts and conflicts reflect the tensions in the lives of people such as those Gardzienice visited, and were consonant with their already established performance aesthetics. This relationship between fieldwork and performances is clarified theoretically by Staniewski's notion of 'naturalisation'.

The process of 'naturalisation' is central to Gardzienice's creative journeys. Staniewski defined this term specifically in a 1990 statement:

> *A proven way of creating theatrical performances through supplementing them with traditional cultural phenomena — the so-called 'naturalisation of the performance'. This is done through artistic Gatherings and Expeditions. Such a direction leads to finding an original artistic expression for great human problems contained not only in literature but in any homogeneous environment.*[16]

The group's use of Russian Orthodox hymns is one example of this process. Such collection of material is part of the naturalisation but many more subtle elements are revealed to the company in the villages. Perhaps the most useful touchstone which Expeditions and Gatherings provide is the direct responses of their rural audiences. They react to songs and theatrical material with honesty and clarity, unclouded by assumptions or preconceptions of what performance should be or can do. I have witnessed this in Gardzienice during performances of *Carmina Burana*. Local villagers who have attended the performance there cried out in surprise followed by immense laughter as Zubrzycka-Gołaj falls backwards (deliberately) from a wardrobe. As such, they stood out clearly from the restrained more urban audience who were also attending. Village audiences set a seal of truth on the work by their litmus test reactions. The most useful of these is perhaps that if they are bored, they will immediately start talking. They thus 'naturalise' or 'make honest' Gardzienice's performances.

Avvakum's strong root in Russian Orthodoxy gives it a clear artistic unity and vision that offsets its non-narrative and poetical complexities. Filipowicz has analysed the performance's abstruseness:

> Avvakum *represents an essentially poetic principle which negates illusionism. Reality in the production is entirely problematic, existing in a constant of destruction and recon-*

struction. This fluid dramatic structure reflects a view of human nature as something infinitely malleable to control and transmutation, and thus succeeds where casual and discursive dramaturgy might fail. The obsessive stream of images is in a process of continuous kaleidoscopic transformation which divests the work of permanence and closure.[17]

In showing the particular example of one man and his fickle, troubled and mutable nature, *Avvakum* questions human behaviour, almost acting as a parable or allegory. The openness of the subject matter is reflected in the form, where songs are important for more than just their words. Their rhythm and texture might vary from moment to moment and their sense might be contradicted by physical action or gesture. Transitions such as that between laughter and tears are explored, of which the latter abound in Avvakum's story of his life. *Avvakum's* complexity and the depth with which it questions human nature are both rooted and validated by its detailed clarity, a result amongst other things of the naturalisation process. The very specific relationship between theatre and society which naturalisation espouses is also evident on a broader scale. The piece is attuned to the early 1980s in Poland in its choice of material, its dialogue between high and low culture and its ambivalence and questioning. Martial Law was a period of confusion, ambiguity and violence which *Avvakum* reflects.

Bakhtin described popular-festive folk forms as constantly evolving and changing, denying absolutist and therefore official stances. 'There is no pure abstract negation in the popular-festive system of images; it tends to embrace both poles of becoming in their contradiction and unity',[18] as Filipowicz interprets it. The performance epitomises this and gains a dynamic energy from this vision, as set, action, people and songs constantly change and return in a different form. In one moment a dead body becomes a battering ram and in the next the martyr becomes a scourge. For Bakhtin such popular-festive images appear concretely in uncrownings, thrashings and mockery which are the main experiences of Avvakum's life. This performance portrays a continually changing, carnivalesque topsy-turvy world rooted in a firm base of belief and passion.

The performers' physical discipline and precision contradict the structural and thematic equivocation and the disjointed sequences. Not one foot seems to be out of place and seemingly dangerous moments abound: an actor falls from a pole to the floor and two bodies slide down stakes, their supports knocked from beneath their slumped bodies. The actors have a unified style of walking, with their long black priestly gowns and dresses hitched up and held gathered at the waist. The bare legs end in big black boots which stride around the space with long steps and fluid bodies. The company simulated the way of moving needed to cross the Siberian landscape through practising on the tundra of Lappland during an Expedition. The eight or so people in the performance (it varies according to the size of the chorus) fill the space with whirling black shapes, climbing up and down the ladders, bringing on carts or moving as a stumbling line of devotees. Before describing the physical action further, more aspects of the mise-en-scene should be detailed, for they are thoroughly integrated with the movement and to a certain extent determine it.

The staging consists primarily of two wooden platforms at opposite ends of the room. These and most other articles were made by local carpenters and seem to belong to life rather than theatre, old, worn and functional as they are. Both platforms are reached by wooden ladders which can be easily removed and which also make double doors. These echo those of the Russian Orthodox church, yet here in the theatre we are behind them in the sacred space usually accessible only to the 'pope'. The platforms are primarily for the chorus yet are also used as both a place to which one can escape and a place from which to preach. When an *anałoyczyk* or lectern is lifted onto the platform Avvakum delivers his sermon from it. There are cart-wheels, poles which can stand in them, (rising into the air as in Breughel's paintings), and objects such as a small cradle, boards with painted icons on them and numerous candles stuck in loaves of round Polish bread. These provide the only source of lighting.

Everything except the platforms and the icons can move and does. The candles are manipulated by the actors to light particular moments and new wooden constructions such as a cart or torture-wheel are built from rearrangements of the elements of the set. Objects have a function beyond their everyday use. A funeral shroud is transformed into a whip. The spatial inversion which places the audience in the forbidden altar area is also a typical example of *mundus inversus* that pervades the whole piece. This staging and use of objects is typically carnivalesque in its flexibility and relativity, where nothing is what it is and everything is open to permutation.

The set was built to fit into the small room in the manor which was formerly a chapel. It is a tight fit and allows only approximately twenty-eight people to sit on benches along two sides and under the larger platform. All are very close to the action. It is also possible to erect the stage in a much larger space as happens when the company tour to towns and cities for festivals. This allows a bigger audience, though Staniewski demands a ceiling limit of 200 people. (They also will not perform for more than three nights in a run, which can be frustrating for promoters and audience alike, yet ensures packed houses). By means of this flexible staging they have performed in numerous churches and historical buildings throughout the world. This very practical search for a new 'natural' environment for the theatre and the rejection of what Staniewski sees as dead theatre spaces, usually provides acoustic and atmospheric support to the performance. It heightens its religiosity and recalls its beginnings in actual songs of worship and rituals. Churches are not directly a 'natural' environment in terms of a rural setting, but they 'naturalise' the performance because of its subject matter. The spirit of theatre can in part be revived, Staniewski believes, by placing it in spaces that were built for spiritual reasons, which in turn remembers the mediaeval sources of European theatre.

The costumes of *Avvakum* are simple and show the style of the performance as an ensemble creation, with actors not playing specific characters. The men have dark gowns as already described and the women have waistcoats and skirts, reminiscent of Slavic folk dress in their shape rather than colour. Different actors play Avvakum and with the uniformity of design, they have the ability to move fluidly in and out of role — this is directly transmitted from actor to actor either by a clear textual sign or a physical emblem such as the handing over of a censer. The distinct relationship between the chorus and the main protagonists is therefore defined by song and positioning, by musically or physically isolating the latter, rather than more overt symbols such as design. The scenography is suggestive and atmospheric and does not try to clarify meaning or narrative. The priests' gowns are not precise replicas but allow the imagination to turn them into peasant or religious garb. This fluidity does however have a firm root in iconography and religious imagery and seems clearly historical rather than contemporary.

The dialogue between 'the chorus and the messenger' is central to Gardzienice's work. The structure of a messenger who brings information to and takes it from the chorus has parallels closer to Poland than the more familiar choral structures of Ancient Greek theatre. The common mode of singing in rural Poland comprises one or two central figures who lead the rest of the chorus but who also have solo moments. The Russian Orthodox service involves the interrelationship between the pope's solo incantations and the chorus, as reflected in *Avvakum*. In Gardzienice's performances the main actors or protagonists may lead the choir and always sing in relation to them. They perhaps start and finish a song with them, while their physical action accompanying the main body of the song is spatially separated from the choir. The performances (particularly the last two productions) have an open choir which can grow or diminish in size. In *Carmina Burana* the choir gathers around a harmonium and its sound can be increased by many additional members, who have included amongst them Polish folk/jazz trio Kwartet Jorgi and myself. The balance between individual etudes and the chorus's songs is central to Gardzienice's practice and allows a large degree of open participation in their work.

The presence of the choir in *Avvakum* creates both a forceful sound and a visually large and active crowd of performers in a small space. The impact of this is particularly noticeable when viewing the performance in the space for which it was first designed, where one feels dangerously close to the hurtling bodies, wheels and candles. This sense of physical danger increases the awe which comes as much from the complex themes and subject matter and juxtaposition of texts as the overwhelming energy and wealth of sounds and images of this short performance.

There is an immediate feeling of silence and overdose when it ends, almost exhaustion. One is enthralled by its seeming danger, its repetitions and its detailed candle lighting, which demands close specific attention. Its density is also mystifying, particularly when the language is not understood. A Korean critic described his response in the following way, which also considers the function of a Gathering after the performance (the translation is poor):

> *though embarrassed a little by this short performance I could get out of the theatre, conjecturing that it might be calculated so that the audience could have time to ease the shock having a cup of tea with friends before going home.*[19]

It is clear that with or without an understanding of the language (the songs are in Old Slavonic which has many similarities to contemporary Polish, though meanings are not clarified by the fast intonation of texts) many are overwhelmed by the performance — on an intellectual level in its mixture of the sacred and profane, and on a visceral level in relation to the physical/visual 'score', to employ Grotowski's terminology.

In simple terms, the performance questions the myth of Poland as a Messianic nation and a suffering, martyred country. Avvakum's martyrdom and sacrifice are not presented as a paradigm of Poland's own history. Rather they show the folly of an egotistical dogged pursuit of nationalistic aims (Nikon's reforms looked for inspiration from the Greek Orthodox church) and the ability of humans to be violent and easily swayed. *Avvakum* strips bare the idea of Poland as a Christian stronghold and therefore Europe's potential saviour and mocks the history of lamentation. It is anti-heroic from Romantic perspectives for Avvakum is not a Romantic version of Mickiewicz's Konrad but a man bravely but foolishly suffering at the hands of an indomitable oppressor. *Avvakum* criticises authority by attacking not only the colonialist Soviet/Russian powers but any absolutist body or school of thought, be it Marxism or the teachings of the Catholic Church. Yet *Avvakum* also shows the individual pursuit of ideals as potentially destructive.

The contrast of opposites again reflects carnivalesque principles, but *Avvakum's* imagery started to move away away from Bakhtin's analysis of carnival, having its roots in religious rather than secular culture. The frequent inversions and stylistic devices remember the carnivalesque but generally the images and inspiration are less popular-festive than in *Evening Spectacle* for example. In the way that *Sorcery* was influenced by *Avvakum*, so was *Avvakum* moulded by the more celebratory spirit of *Carmina Burana*.

With its consummate energy, *Avvakum* forces highly personal responses on a direct emotional level from its audience, bypassing rational responses with its complexity and richness. Yet *Avvakum's* raw emotion belongs to the contrasts and extremism of the Martial Law period. In its references to Russian Orthodoxy it is a cry against Poland's introverted nationalism, as well as being related clearly to the oppression during the time of its creation. The fact that the company has found more humour in the performance since I first saw it in 1989 shows the greater distance with which Martial Law and Soviet oppression are now viewed. The notion of a satirical Romantic hero also has less currency when Romanticism has been rejected as a frame of reference. Watching *Avvakum* in the 1990s, it seems to have moved from being a topical commentary to a historical slice of Poland's and Gardzienice's history. Performances about oppression, flight and exile seem retrospective in post-1989 Poland. *Avvakum*'s long life perhaps made it inevitable that its subject matter and tone would become outdated. Radical political changes merely hastened this process. Yet in spite of these questions about its context, *Avvakum* remains a rich, dynamic monument to Gardzienice's vision and unique approach to creating performances.

Carmina Burana

Carmina Burana evolved over several years and was premiered in November 1990. The piece was designed for the large theatre hall in Gardzienice's newly restored building, whose floor was not completed until May 1990. The other downstairs rooms of the *oficyna* were not ready until a few months later. The performance, on a practical level at least, had to wait until building-work rendered the space usable as a theatre. However, almost the entire musical score of *Carmina Burana* was sung through in Italy in July 1990 in the chapel of San Pietro Alle Stinche. This was just one of many stages in the complex and long creation of this piece. Since 1990 it has played throughout Poland and at international festivals but only in autumn 1992 did it seem to have reached 'completion'. In spite of the apparent conclusion to the creative process which a premiere signals, new elements and sections continued to be added. During 1992 these additions became less radical as the year progressed, eventually related to integrating new choir or acting members rather than developing material. The most intense times of creativity for the production were during 1989 and 1990. When I worked with the company in Gardzienice in the winter that bridged these years there were daily rehearsals where an excess of material was made. Much of this was later discarded or subsumed, as is often the case in the early stages of a creative process. In this instance the amount of 'waste' was huge, reflecting the long, intense rehearsal period.

    Carmina Burana's musical inspiration comes from the thirteenth century Carmina Burana song cycle, which was written mainly by anonymous clerks and wandering scholars or Goliards — the etymology is uncertain but perhaps the name describes disciples and followers of the legendary bishop Golias who became a celebrated songwriter. It contains a mixture of secular and a few religious songs from several countries, in both Latin, the language then of officialdom and the church, and German, the native language of the people of Bavaria. This area, where the two hundred or so songs it comprises were collected, is more specifically called Beuren (hence Carmina Burana — songs of Beuren). The Codex Burana, as the whole collection is called, moves through a vast range of emotions and styles, from erotic and chaste love homages to bawdy drinking songs. Comparable with this and with the subject matter of *Avvakum, Carmina Burana* has a similar scope, showing the power of conflicting aspirations, the contradictory nature of the world and the fragility of human existence. The human condition is exemplified nowhere more clearly than in the Codex song 'O Fortuna' about fickle Fortune, personified on her perpetually revolving wheel. Gardzienice use a range of songs from the Codex, from this one to the cynical ' Ecce Torpet Probitas' — "Look around you — integrity is in a coma, / Virtue dead and buried." This music is best known today through composer Carl Orff's 1937 interpretation. Gardzienice selected, arranged and developed the music under the direction of Tomasz Rodowicz with Maciej Rychły of Kwartet Jorgi.

The narrative core of the performance comes from the Celtic story of 'Tristan and Isolde', which was originally transcribed by the enigmatic figure of Thomas, probably in the twelfth century. It is better known through many other interpretations, from Gottfried von Strassburg's epic romance to Wagner's operatic version. It is a simple and familiar story, concerning a magic potion which is unwittingly drunk, causing two young courtiers, Tristan and Isolde, to fall in love. To fulfill their passion they must defy Isolde's official suitor King Mark and the story follows this triangular conflict. It shares many elements with other ancient European stories: a magic love potion, banished lovers, the noble warrior pursued by his friend of higher status and an untimely and eventually shared death, like that in Shakespeare's *Romeo and Juliet*.

This story is used by Gardzienice not as triangular narrative, but to show the fickle nature of love through allegorical events. It provides a loose framework of episodes, which include Tristan's madness, his wooing of Isolde on the boat and the anger of King Mark. In the performance it is not easy to discern such moments, so initially the characters introduce themselves to ease confusion: Tristan, the older and younger Isoldes, King Mark, Merlin and his wife Vivien (these two are not part of the original story and are developed from the Arthurian legends). Some parts of the written stories are intact, usually delivered as dialogue, as in the scene depicting Tristan's feigned madness. Some images are directly transposed, like the ominous black sail of the boat on which Tristan and Isolde spin round at the climax of the performance. Generally the original narrative is split up into isolated moments and action sequences, reflecting the contrasting and eternally interwoven themes of love and war.

Within and between sections of the story, other texts are used. These range from Solomon's 'Song of Songs' in the Bible — 'Stay me with flagons, comfort me with apples: for I am sick of love . . . Thou hast ravished my heart' — to the section in *Macbeth* (Act One, Scene Seven) concerning Duncan's murder — 'If it were done when 't is done, then t'were well / It were done quickly'. The songs' lyrics are also part of the audible text: The Pilgrim Fathers' song — 'He dies, the friend of sinners dies / Lo, Salam's daughters weep around' — accompanies a section called 'the domestic war'. This is presented as a 'battle of the sexes' and is figuratively and physically suggested. Accompanied by action, both sung and spoken texts do not expound the narrative or characters' behaviour, but contribute to the layers of meaning through careful structuring — a form of audio-montage. In spite of the ensuing complexity and richness, the characters' progression and from this a sense of the narrative is clearer and more accessible in *Carmina Burana* than it is in *Avvakum*.

The roles of Merlin and Vivien cast objective light on the intimate relationship between Tristan and Isolde. As well as physical and vocal interactions with the others, when they take on a choral rather than character-specific relationship, they show a more archetypical portrayal of male / female relationships than that of Tristan and Isolde. They enact the fore-mentioned scene from *Macbeth* with Gołaj manipulating Corrigan as his puppet wife, giving her voice Judy's shrillness with all the coarseness of a Punch and Judy puppet show. The choir leader accompanies this with fairground organ music. Such moments allude in a popular performance style to the stereotypical battle of the sexes. Merlin and Vivien are low culture down-to-earth characters, in contrast to the poetic romantics Tristan and Isolde. If one is aware of the mythological and literary interpretations of Merlin and Vivien, the *Macbeth* sequence is underscored by the knowledge that she entranced him with love. His physical domination over her thus becomes ironic. If one is not aware of such literary complexities the characters seem to be simple representations, commenting on events and adding to the choral action.

Merlin is archetypical for he is also provocateur and trickster and the animator of the performance. Gołaj had a more objective role than the other performers in developing the performance, overseeing the physical sequences. This is evident in his stage role. At the start of the performance, he opens the main doors and leads on a real horse. He later lights the candles, opens the wardrobe doors and moves the piece on with interruptions and shouted commands. In his black magician's cape, he scuttles like a spider around the stage with his wife. His ego is revealed in his quickly intoned monologue with the emphasis always on the personal pronoun. He spews forth his litany of self-inflation:

> *Ja byłem w wielu ksztaltach zanim mnie uwolniono . . .*
> *Ja byłem z moim Panem w niebiesiech, ja nosiłem*
> *sztandar / I appeared in many shapes*
> *before I was freed . . . I was with my God in the heavens,*
> *I was the flag bearer.*[20]

Gołaj sees his role as representing that element in all of us which pays no heed to the existence of others and hence eschews mutuality.

This selfish demi-God is in antithesis to the collective nature of the choir. At one stage in the rehearsal process, Staniewski asked me to select from the Tristan and Isolde texts all the sentences that started with 'I'. The idea now appears in this condensed speech, which comes from the thirteenth century mythological collection of Welsh Arthurian stories the *Book of Taliesin*. This is one of the more simply presented moments of the performance, a blunt intrusion of the ego, audibly disharmonious in contrast to the choir's musicality. Staniewski and Gołaj were inspired by Jung's writing on the trickster myth,[21] which describes the trickster as a shadow in civilised society, visible in a consciousness of superstition, mischief and the animalistic side of human behaviour. Merlin recalls this suppressed instinct in us. By opening the doors of the theatre space Gołaj/Merlin is drawing us into the trickster's carnivalesque world.

When the piece is performed in Gardzienice, audience members are ushered in by Staniewski and helpers and individually shown to a place in the left or right set of old church pews, facing the main stage area. There is a central passage-way between these four rows of seats, running toward the back of the theatre (Staniewski has proudly called it his 'church'). Level with the last row of pews is a harmonium on a raised rostrum — the place for the choir and their leader. At the main 'altar' end of the large hall is a platform of rostra by which stand two large wardrobes, one on each side, and a giant wheel of fortune which can be spun round by a water mill-wheel mechanism. Under these rostra is stored a huge half-barrel with a removable lid, which can be wheeled out into the central stage area, between the platform and audience. There are ladders leading up from the rostra to the tops of the cupboards and King Mark's stool is at the pinnacle of the set, a precarious ledge above the wheel. Stage-left, in one wall of the building, between the cupboard and the first row of pews, are two large doors which open out onto the meadows. The whole is lit by two small electric lanterns and candles dotted around the set and building. There is a bright soft glow over all events though at one point this is extinguished to create a total blackout for the musical sequence entitled 'The Musician's Hell'. As with *Avvakum* much of the set was built by local craftsmen, yet its scale is larger and more rambling.

The scenography provides flexibility of levels and staging and means that action is closely integrated with the set. At one point Tristan is strapped to the wheel and spun round with frightening velocity as fools would have been on the sixteenth century Nürnberg carnival wheel, as part of a depiction of hell. Isolde the Elder falls backwards off a cupboard and is suspended from the top of it by her feet. A variety of levels are used with King Mark looking down on the action from his palace perch. The floor is spacious enough for acrobatic and physical sequences such as the 'war'. The doors of the two wardrobes seem magically to open and close, and tableaux inside them are revealed and then disappear. The half-barrel becomes a boat, a grave and a movable mini-stage. The scenography is often surprising, but perhaps the most impressive and simple aspect of the design is the potential offered by the building itself, with doors that lead directly outside.

At the beginning of the performance the doors are thrown open for Merlin to lead in a cart horse, a gesture of empathy with nature and a stunning theatrical moment. Later the audience is signalled to leave by these doors and spectators must walk across the grass into the black night. These doors 'naturalise' the act of attending a performance by acknowledging the rural surroundings. The presence of the horse sets a magical tone yet is also a theatricalisation of one small part of nature. The dimension this entrance and its use adds to the performance is difficult to describe, sensory and suggestive as it is. This effect is of course lost when the performance tours, though another horse was used by the company for the 1992 European Culture Festival in Cracow.

One of the main achievements of *Carmina Burana* is the actors' performances, which can be dynamic and lyrical. The company weave their way with dexterity and physical ease through demanding action and vocal sequences. Intense concentration is needed to follow the nonnarrative sequence and find a secure path through the often illogical selection of texts. There are fast shifts in musical levels of pitch and tone and in energy quality, demanding stamina and extreme physical awareness. A complex Georgian song is accompanied by Tristan 'dancing' with his two Isoldes, first one, then both and then just the second. Their balance is perfect, the difficult rhythm is controlled and great strength, trust and understanding are revealed. Technically precise as well as aesthetically thrilling, they accurately denote the ache and ardor of intense love. The actors work together with split-second timing, rhythmically and melodically in tune with the choir, or a monologue or a spoken or sung duet. There are many layers in each moment of the performance, the distillation of years of rehearsal and training, and the actors' attention and energy can never flag. If they do, Staniewski, located near the choir, will either urge on the action or inject a shout of admonishment.

Carmina Burana has a more playful mood than *Avvakum*. There is physical space between the audience and the actors and between the actors themselves, there is variety in the musical pace and tone, and the subject matter is handled gently, reflecting the lighter side of the amorous material. There are even one or two moments of humour, as when Mark and Tristan debate their rights to Isolde's body as two quack doctors in a Latin song — 'Ego Sum Abbas'. The performance is not as provocative as *Avvakum*, with less violent and contradictory imagery, and is also on a much larger scale, in the scope of the content, its staging, its allusions and its general presentation. When the company perform in Gardzienice, there is a long sequence of events: firstly *Avvakum* with numbers limited to twenty eight and then *Carmina Burana* for sixty people after a break for tea. This 'Marathon', as Staniewski calls it, highlights the contrasting atmosphere between the two performances.

In Gardzienice the audience sit in restrictive pews which prohibit their visual contact with the choir, reflecting the arrangement for a church. The openness of both the space and the lighting can diffuse the focus, which is particularly noticeable after witnessing the precision of *Avvakum's* design and action. The unwieldy choir also creates problems. It is cumbersome and can slow the pace. Tensions then arise between choir members and the full-time members of the company. This is sometimes revealed in performance by a musical disharmony between the performers and the choir, which is not helped by the depth of the playing area. On tour, *Carmina Burana* suffers from a lack of voices, particularly when performed in large spaces such as churches. The lack of motivation in the choir with whom I sang in England in 1992 deeply troubled the morale of the core of the ensemble, perhaps undermining their nightly efforts and years of training. The choir was mostly made up of very young newcomers who had joined after the previous team disbanded at the end of a tour of Sweden. The presence of performers who do not understand or adhere to Gardzienice's philosophy and practice, undermines the ideal of a specifically trained close-knit ensemble. The discipline Staniewski expects of all his performers seemed to unsettle the relatively inexperienced choir members, some of whom were from musical rather than theatrical backgrounds and who had been recruited at short notice to undertake a long foreign tour.

Avvakum's songs are rooted in a particular culture and religion, whereas *Carmina Burana's* music is eclectic, coming from the Codex Burana (and particularly Renee Clemencic's lively arrangements), but also from many other places, including Britain, Poland, Scandinavia, Georgia and Greece. The final song *'Eksomologeisthe to kyrio'* is from the religious enclaves of Mount Athos which Staniewski visited. The music seems almost random, chosen according to the director's vision. Textual choices reflect this diversity, taken from different retellings of the central myth (in particular Hilaire Belloc's poetical translation of Bedier's version)[22] and from several other secular and religious sources. The musical heterogeneity points to Gardzienice's wider travels and the larger number of foreigners who have visited or worked with them during the creation of this performance. It represents a shift from village to town, from found rural dialogue to Shakespeare, and from cultural specificity to multi-cultural diversity.

Kolankiewicz has observed that showing the two performances together reveals 'the sublimation of folk culture and the re-grounding of high culture.'[23] Having performed humble Avvakum's quest for Godliness on earth, the company show the baser instincts of love-struck kings and courtiers, recognising love as a leveller of all people. Yet this 're-grounding' is a theoretical construct and seems to refer mostly to the use of source materials. The physical action of the performance has not undergone a naturalisation process to the extent that the previous performances did. Only twice during the later development of the performance (after its premiere in 1991 and 1992), did Gardzienice lead major rural Expeditions, when they visited Huculszczysna (an area inhabited by the Huculs, early settlers in the Ukrainian Carpathian mountains). Partly because of this minimal fieldwork, there are few elements of native culture in the performance. Gardzienice now use more sources from higher culture than lower culture. The characters of *Carmina Burana* are nobles from a courtly genre, who are in love rather than lusting. Only Merlin and Vivien reveal Bakhtin's 'lower material bodily stratum' with their moments in a more popular performance style. The company has thus distanced itself from popular-festive and rural imagery and replaced it with idioms from higher culture.

This is linked in part to Gardzienice's wider use of cultural sources. They no longer seem to be an informal Slavic 'National theatre', inspired by Mickiewicz's writings on the nature of Slavic arts. *Carmina Burana* has few references to Slavic culture, the songs coming predominantly from Western Europe and the texts from Celtic and British literature and the Bible. During the creation of the performance and before its premiere there was a very brief rural Expedition in Italy to the Chianti district where Gardzienice first performed *Sorcery*, and where *Carmina Burana's* musical score was first sung. Research excursions were also made in England to visit places mentioned in *Tristan and Isolde* such as Tintagel but these were by no means Expeditions. *Carmina Burana* is more literarily referential than previous performances, reflecting in part the culture of the countries where research took place and from which source materials came.

Such criteria do not mean that the performance is weak for it has many beautiful moments. *Carmina Burana* is lyrical and moving, rousing and comic, is paced with variety and speed and builds to a thrilling conclusion. It has a dynamic physical score and acrobatic sequences. This was reflected by its reception in January 1992 at the Warsaw Theatre Meetings. In *Gazeta Wyborcza*,[24] a national daily newspaper, a critic friendly to Gardzienice hailed them as the most successful theatre company in Poland, and in *Teatr* magazine, *Carmina Burana* was named the best performance of 1991. Weaknesses with the performance relate mostly to the production on tour and the role of the choir, exacerbated by the extreme complexity and difficulty of the music. The use of space is not as focused as that in *Avvakum* and does not fully support the singing. Yet the performance gains from its wider range of colours and music and tones, and the pleasure it induces through laughter.

Carmina Burana reveals a clear stylistic departure from the tone and subject matter of *Avvakum* and charts difficult to define territory. Towards the beginning of their work on *Carmina Burana*, Staniewski described the piece in the following way:

its theme is an allegorical image of a human being in an age of transition. It is a vision of man suspended between two cultures (pagan and Christian). And so the Middle Ages became a metaphor of man's condition in our contemporary world. Both Arch poet and Goliard, evolving out of two cultures — the 'high' and the 'low' one — preferred to identify themselves with neither of them. They constituted a unique 'Wandering order' — (Ordo Vagorum). It was said that 'they died excommunicated by the church, but created great poetry and great scandals'.[25]

This was written for Gardzienice's 1989 British tour programme but reappeared for the performances of *Carmina Burana* in Cracow in May 1991. This description reveals the inspirational base to the production but little of such notion is left in the performance, for these words look back to the man Avvakum rather than forward to the people Tristan and Isolde. The Goliards remain only in their songs and therefore the contrasting emotions and conflict in their material rather than directly as a theme or as characters.

Polish critic Marek Zagańczyk highlights the contemporary relevance of the production, with reference to the transitional age when the Carmina Burana songs were compiled — 'the autumn of of the Middle Ages'.[26] He relates that time to Poland's present passage from an absolutist ideology to a free-market system, and the feeling of suspension that many now feel. To me the performance seems timeless rather than historical, as Staniewski has revealed by saying lightheartedly but with underlying truth: 'the production is about love, in other words about nothing'.[27] Whatever connections one may search for between the performance and real life, Gardzienice's presentations have moved from the specific and political to the mythological and universal, from the more objective to the personal. Theatre criticism has the difficult task of keeping up with such changes and divorcing itself from previous obsessions with history and the politicisation of Polish theatre.

Both Zagańczyk and Majcherek analyse Gardzienice's development in articles whose titles in translation approximately mean 'Between East and West'. In these they seem to want to relocate Polish theatre by asserting its and Gardzienice's position in the midst of Western culture. Such approaches may undermine the group's firmly established identity and unique qualities. The naming of new values and frameworks by critics can relegate to history former virtues and conditions that have created internationally renowned groups such as Gardzienice. While the two critics cited are too intelligent to wholeheartedly go along this path of glamourising Western practices, the tendencies that exist even in their works show broader potentially destructive trends and show the difficulties theatre criticism now faces in renegotiating the rules of engagement.

In stating how theatre should develop one is in danger of restricting its future development. Artists do not need prescriptive rules in the present artistic confusion. This could imply a return to the restrictions that existed in the worst years of Stalinist control in Poland. Yet how can Polish critics help artists benefit from this major reassessment of their identity, thus keeping the wheat and disregarding the chaff? There may be important Western examples of practice which artists could adopt, like very different attitudes to women, which will enrich their already firm base. Critics can help artists see what is specific to them and what is valuable and help clarify how to keep hold of that. Unfortunately finances often make such choices redundant. Money is one of the most pressing problems now facing artists in Poland as Zygmunt Hubner indicated to *New Theatre Quarterly* readers: 'I am speaking about money, because unfortunately it is money and not art that worries us most.'[28] Money has its own rhythm and does not always allow time to reflect or hesitate. The age of Polish theatre as a commercial industry rather than a political agent has just begun.

7

EUROPEAN PARALLELS – FUTURE MODELS

By examining the activities of other European theatre practitioners, one can assess Gardzienice's practice in a broader geographical and historical context. The Romantic vision of working creatively in a natural environment for a new audience away from the deprivation of urban society has been pursued by many before Gardzienice. One can trace this desire through the work of Stanislavski, Jacques Copeau, Peter Brook, Eugenio Barba, Tadashi Suzuki and of course Grotowski, most noticeably during his paratheatrical explorations. I will touch briefly on the work of these practitioners, some only in passing, with the exception of Grotowski who has already been discussed. None have pursued this quest to such an extent and as consistently as Staniewski, with the exception perhaps of Jacques Copeau. These examples reveal Gardzienice's unique approach and suggest possible models of development for their future.

Staniewski rarely acknowledges the example of these directors and has never mentioned Copeau's mission to build a rural base. Vakhtangov is one of the few historical sources to which Gardzienice refer as theatrical inspiration, a connection which was particularly strong during the company's early existence. I hope to shed light on the broad sweep of Gardzienice's development since their foundation in order to posit some possible future avenues, siting their quest for a 'new natural environment for the theatre' within a Romantic field of vision. By initially analysing their relationship to Vakhtangov one can see how their work has moved away from his espousal of a relationship with a specific audience to a wider public and sphere of influence.

A brief statement by the Armenian born Evgeny Vakhtangov (1883–1922) introduced Gardzienice's first artistic manifesto, printed and privately distributed in 1978. His influence on Gardzienice is not explicit for little has been said or written about it beyond this quotation, but he seems to be a source of inspiration for the company. This empathy with Vakhtangov's principles belongs more to the earlier rural touring period rather than the more recent phase of their activities. Few correlations between Staniewski's and Vakhtangov's work are now perceptible.

Vakhtangov was a student of Stanislavski's (1863–1938) at the start of this century. After acting in many roles he became a director, developing a style which he called 'imaginative realism'.[1] Towards the end of his life he went so far as to reject Stanislavski's approach, (though he always acknowledged his great debt to him), writing 'May naturalism in the theatre die!'.[2] His emphasis on process and actor development meant that up to three years might be spent on realising a production. The individual and group creations were formed and analysed with minute precision. Each performance had its own distinctive style and he received much acclaim for them. His determined application to a few pieces rather than an emphasis on building a large repertoire and his demand for highly trained performers are both priorities of Gardzienice's work.

Vakhtangov was invited to work for a Jewish theatre and became guest director at Moscow's Hebrew-language theatre, the Habima. This was founded in 1917 with Stanislavski as advisor and still operates today in Israel. Vakhtangov worked for three years with the company on the celebrated production of Anski's *The Dybbuk* (1922). The temperament at the Habima reflected and was in part moulded by Vakhtangov's seriousness and commitment: 'The Habima company ... bound themselves together by ties in a closed circle and separated themselves from the rest of the theatrical world'.[3] He also directed productions in his own studio, the Vakhtangov Studio in Moscow, under the auspices of Stanislavski. In 1920 it was renamed the Third Art Theatre Studio and later became the Vakhtangov Theatre. Vakhtangov's last years were plagued by his fight against cancer and he worked passionately in spite of great pain.

It is vital when considering Vakhtangov's relation to Gardzienice to understand the political context in which he operated and to sketch the compatibility of his revolutionary allegiances with his artistic criteria. He lived for only five years after the October Revolution, yet he championed its goals and the aim of empowering the people, accordingly realigning his theatre. Like Tairov (1885–1950) and other young Russian directors who followed the explorations of Meyerhold (1874–1940) and such inspirational pieces as *The Fairground Booth* (1906), Vakhtangov turned to popular forms such as circus and pageants. In this way the festive spirit of theatre could be revived, suitable for the radically altered times:

> *If the artist wants to create something 'new', to go on creating after the Revolution has come, he must do so 'together' with the people. Not for them, not on their behalf, not outside them, but together with them. In order to create something new and to be victorious, the artist needs, just like Antaeus, contact with the earth. The people are this earth.*[4]

This meant familiarity with popular forms and breaking away from the theatrical and hence political limitations of Stanislavskian 'fourth-wall' drama. To directors such as Vakhtangov and other protégés of Stanislavski, that form was outmoded and for a minority interest. Reflecting aspirations concomitant with the Revolution, they wished to break with conformity and speak to a wider audience. Gar-

dzienice reflected and interpreted Vakhtangov's views and his search for new audiences and forms according to their context: by locating themselves and their fieldwork in rural areas; by finding fresh artistic impetus form villagers in terms of folk
influences; and by developing new creative processes amongst the people in
Expeditions and Gatherings. They were looking for meeting points between high
and low culture, as they described it. Their own creations used folk songs and villagers' dialogue and their 'earth' was the muddy roads and paths into Polish villages. In this way they literally worked 'together with the people' as Vakhtangov
espoused, defying restrictive Communist practices and preconditions.

According to Vakhtangov such contact could reveal the inherent value of
art. He believed that this respect for the people and connection with them should
not prioritise experimentation at the expense of accessibility. Rather it should
encourage openness in reassessing tired forms for a privileged minority. Likewise,
Gardzienice did not want to entertain by appropriating popular models, but to
find new forms and approaches and challenge themselves and their audiences. For
Vakhtangov as for Staniewski this had to stem from contact with the people that
went deeper than just meeting them as an audience. Vakhtangov:

> *That which is not overheard within the popular soul, that which is not divined within the
> popular heart, can never be of long-term value. One must go round listening to the people.
> One must melt into the crowd and feel its pulse. One must imbibe creative strength from
> the people. One must contemplate the people with one's whole creative being.*[5]

Vakhtangov challenged and developed the achievements of his antecedents. One
can understand how Vakhtangov became a vital, stimulating mentor for Gardzienice in their formative years, after Staniewski had just left the rarified atmosphere of Grotowski's paratheatrical work.

Vakhtangov's devotion and patient practice seem to be qualities that were
inherent in Gardzienice's own formerly more isolated and extreme existence. Their
dogged perseverance in their first five years in difficult conditions and during
Martial Law echo Vakhtangov's unbridled commitment and energy. However, their
'closed circle' has progressively widened as the specific intimacy of their relationship to Slavic culture has diminished. Since the Second World War Polish artists
have continually sought ties with Western artists, particularly in France and Britain, and now such connections are much more possible on an economic as well as
cultural level. One sees this in Gardzienice's sustained contact with the Royal
Shakespeare Company. In these more open circles the contact with a specific social
strata has become subordinated to demands such as international touring and
training projects. Gardzienice may be based in a village but financial necessity often
forces them abroad for long periods. They now work to the rhythm of another
pulse.

Vakhtangov sought inspiration from the people but this did not necessarily mean rural audiences. Stanislavski pursued the idea of rural summer rehearsals in a barn in Pushkino, some twenty miles from Moscow, whilst preparing for the first season of the Moscow Art Theatre. This allowed sustained rehearsals and a sense of community to be nurtured, yet it was only for the preparation of work rather than its presentation, which brought Stanislavski back to Moscow. Gardzienice seemed to draw on the example of Vakhtangov's search to find new forms and new audiences rather than Stanislavski's model of rural rehearsals. Staniewski's search for a new natural environment was uniquely aligned to the Polish situation and the post-war industrialisation of Poland and its rural culture. However, others have fulfilled similar objectives to Staniewski's rural mission to a much greater extent than either Vakhtangov or Stanislavki.

Direct connections can be made between Staniewski and the French director Jacques Copeau (1879–1947), for they have shared similar preoccupations — notably the importance of a rural environment for performance and training and the value of contact with rural audiences. The example of Copeau sheds light on the strength of Staniewski's own achievements and sketches possible future problems for the company which Copeau himself never reconciled. It clarifies the specific difficulties for theatre artists of sustaining the Romantic vision of working in an undeveloped rural environment.

In pre-First World War Europe, Copeau was renowned as a theatre critic who condemned the whims and artificialities of the commercial theatre. In 1913 he founded the small Théâtre du Vieux-Colombier in Paris and started to direct. The company's initial success was stifled by the outbreak of the First World War. He then directed French actors for a year and a half in the Garrick Theatre in New York. In 1919, with the war over, the company returned home to Paris for five years where they established a world-wide reputation for innovative small-scale productions. During this period Copeau founded and ran the Vieux-Colombier School for actor training, whilst directing productions in the theatre. This gradually took precedence for Copeau and in 1924 he moved the school to the countryside in Burgundy to focus their explorations. This move came at the same time as his conversion to Catholicism. The group (which became known as Les Copiaus or little Copeau's in dialect) created several performances under Copeau's guidance before they disbanded in 1929. Copeau then returned to his writing, directing only a few more productions before his death in 1947. Etienne Decroux and Michel Saint-Denis, Copeau's nephew, received their initial training with Copeau. The latter's work at the Old Vic Theatre School in London just after the Second World War was to have a transforming effect on British actor training, emphasising extensive control of physical expressivity using forms such as mime and mask-work. Traditions established by Copeau continue in France today in the schools of teachers like Jacques Lecoq, who trained with Copeau's son-in-law Jean Dasté. From this base

Copeau's influence has spread across Europe to embrace British companies like Théâtre de Complicité, whose founders trained at the Lecoq school in Paris.

Copeau expressed continual frustration with actors who could not be open, spontaneous and simple on stage. He constantly battled against their egos and their desire for gratification, lamenting their lack of commitment and passion, both of which he felt he possessed. To this end he chose, like Staniewski, to painstakingly retrain a group of actors who were selected for their personal qualities as much for evidence of underlying talent. He initially set up rigorous physical, mental and educational training schedules to run alongside rehearsals. These could only be fully realised when he set up his 'school in the country.'

The realignment of priorities which Copeau sought and his rejection of the established theatre could be achieved in part through a closer relationship to nature. He chose to leave urban distractions to make a break with theatrical conventions and thus to cut through artifice in the theatre. When performing in Paris he took his actors to exercise in the garden of his house in Limon and after performing in New York they retreated to rehearse in rural New Jersey. One anonymous Parisian critic observed the effects of this process:

> Outdoor life sets the stamp of truth on their work; theatricalisms which spring to life behind the footlights wither in the sunshine. Here is no coaching for a performance, but the growth of a vital thing.[6]

In spite of the successful stimulus of such exposure, his rural school could not be a full-time undertaking because of the group's urban commitments and performances. Copeau continually struggled between presenting a large repertoire for a general public and more rarified, closed developmental work with a 'brotherhood', as he described his ensemble. In order to fully explore the potential of the latter option, he closed his theatre in Paris and in 1924 established a permanent base for his company in the French countryside. Copeau's continued endeavours to raise money for this venture shadowed him during the life of the school. He often left his group, raising finances, giving lectures and even directing in France and New York. Rudlin has attributed this in part to Copeau's own need for gratification and worldwide recognition as well as to financial considerations.[7]

In Burgundy the group hoped to nurture a close relationship with local people. Copeau looked for a vivid contact and a raw, intuitive audience in contrast to the Parisian spectator who attended the theatre out of a sense of duty or fashion. Their performance material assimilated local sources, be they tales, myths or ideas from observing local villagers. Ultimately this was in order to revivify French theatre by remembering its roots in rural culture. Accordingly their performances had vitality and a local flavour, but above all the environment seemed healthy for the group. Away from the city's theatre circles, Copeau's ensemble could flourish as an isolated, independent unit, enthused with the vitality visible in rural celebrations, as Rudlin has noted:

> *The spirit and natural energy of the country festivals (in which the actors both participated and then, at other times, were able to recreate through their own performances) was best expressed in works that resulted from the collective creation of the whole troupe.*[8]

Some of these approached the atmosphere and style of Greek theatrical events. The language Copeau employed approximates Vakhtangov's own priorities and expressions:

> *Let its tragedy begin with choral chants. Let its comedy begin with gatherings and festivals, embellished with songs and local farces, inspired by the images of characters known in the area. (...) At least they will have grown out of the people for whom they were made, they will have been renewed, refreshed at the very source and will have developed organically naturally. They will be truly new because they will be truly living.*[9]

Les Copiaus developed their own Commedia style, indebted to Moliere, local people and regional influences and in part continuing the traditions of Commedia del' Arte. They created an extensive rough and ready, farcical repertoire using simple masks, which they toured to village market places.

In 1929 Copeau disbanded this rural school. His intense energy and commitment, fuelled by his increasingly devout Catholicism, had overpowered his ensemble, resulting in its collapse. The actors were impatient for progress which outpaced Copeau's slower exploratory rhythm. His regular absences and his ensuing problems in keeping control from both an emotional and practical distance created insoluble tensions. Rudlin has pinpointed some of these. The fact that there was a

> *schism over the proper relationship between work and leisure activities is indicative not only of a breakdown in communication between Copeau and the Copiaus, but also perhaps within Copeau's own psyche. Eric Bentley felt that this attempt to monasticise the creative life was the true chimera of which Gide had spoken: 'One suspects that the theatrical impulse to exhibitionism and self-display and the religious impulse to seclusion and self-denial are fundamentally opposite'.*[10]

Rudlin sees the essential issue as the paradox of attempting to create a 'public monastery' for a performance group. Copeau's use of the word 'brotherhood' points to this dichotomy.

Copeau's religious fervour and persistence and Vakhtangov's dogged passion have some connection to Staniewski's sense of mission. The latter was seemingly driven by his opposition to Communism. His reaction against Communist cultural policies possibly gave him the required intensity to feed his work, in a similar way that Copeau was initially fired by his reaction against the Parisian theatre style. Such a hypothesis, which is impossible to fully corroborate, highlights the difficulties Gardzienice are currently facing. The tensions between the public and the private, the open and the closed are a serious challenge to Gardzienice in an increasingly open society. The example of Copeau shows the strength of Staniewski's achievement to date, with the remarkable existence of his group and a stable core of collaborators since 1977. Yet how solid can a group mission and vision remain when a company becomes public 'state' property and celebrated on an international level? The example of Copeau also raises the question of whether there is such a thing as a collective vision in a group like Gardzienice or whether everyone is motivated by singular director-led inspiration. Was Copeau's increasing intrenchment in the Catholic faith bought on by the trials of his mission? If it was, does it have an equivalent in Staniewski, or is it purely a matter of personality? These questions cannot yet be answered.

One director who initially led Expeditions to villages, but who has since sought inspiration in a wider intercultural field among theatre practitioners is Eugenio Barba. His work connects with Staniewski's along several axes, in part because of a working relationship with Grotowski. His avid interest in Eastern culture developed during his time with Grotowski, whose work he observed for three years in the early 1960s. In 1964 Barba travelled in India researching traditional dance/drama forms, and consequently in Poland he transformed elements of Kathakali exercises for the Laboratory's own system of actor training. He then continued this research with his group Odin Teatret. Brief comparison with Odin's practice is useful for several reasons: the Artistic Directors of both companies initially collaborated with Grotowski; both groups have travelled to remote ethnic minorities to collect material as well as to perform; both have comprised a strong core of group members for more than a decade and have evolved a specialised process of actor training; the company is still active today, combining performances at international venues with research, conferences, training programmes and publications. The fact that Barba has written extensively about his company's work allows a form of access to their rural activities which is useful in light of the lack of material on Gardzienice's fieldwork. Barba's language highlights Staniewski's own Romanticism, as it is rooted in technical theatrical issues and political concerns.

Odin Teatret was founded in Oslo in 1964 and with Barba as Artistic Director used untrained, non-professional actors rejected from conventional drama schools. In the mid 1970s Barba started to intensify his research into rural folk culture and marginal communities. Himself an unusual cultural mixture, (born in Italy in 1936, he emigrated to Norway in 1954 and then lived in Poland for four years) he was fascinated by still intact 'floating islands'.[11] This is what he called marginalised, isolated places which possess a vivid sense of their cultural identity.

He led several projects to make contact with such 'islands' initially in villages in
the poor mountain area of southern Italy, where Gardzienice have also been. His
company communicated primarily through song and 'dance' which for Odin actors
meant exercise sequences. From these contacts Barba developed his notion of 'barter' theatre. This operates on the premise that activity in a village can stimulate
local songs, dances and stories:

> *This was the barter; we did not give our goods away nor did they give theirs. Both parts
> went away with more than they brought. And in spite of our diversity, we confronted
> each other, defining ourselves through our own cultural backgrounds.*[12]

They were not searching for organised folk choirs and experts, but hidden and
untamed, unofficial aspects of a particular region's culture. Like Gardzienice they
were operating in an informal, unbureaucratic way which cut through artificiality
and the effects of cultural manipulation.

As in Staniewski's rural Poland, the places Odin visited were declining,
with people torn between their traditional agrarian world and a pervasive technological urban one. Young and old were dislocated by their awareness of the fast-
paced changes around them and the draw of the cities, problems exacerbated by
economic necessity. Odin's performances could serve a practical, social function
of temporarily fusing the villagers and making them reassert their identity, as Barba
has noted:

> *We wanted them to answer us with their own voice, their own language, that which still
> binds them together and makes them strong, although slowly disintegrating: their cul-
> ture, a culture which does not divide but unites.*[13]

Such meetings could also bring benefits on a practical level as demonstrated by
the instance of the creation of a local library when villagers brought and offered a
book as entrance fee to an Odin performance. Barter attempted to prioritise and
show the various possibilities of cultural expression.

When Odin's activity in rural areas became most concrete it could have
political value in challenging assumptions, established networks and apathy.
Through the conflict and tension of their interaction and in the friction of the differences between two cultures came the sparks of change. Barba was fully aware of the
implications of this. He employed methods and theories that were trying to be
nonoppressive and noncolonialist. The difficulties of this were perhaps most evident
in their journey to the Amazon and the disappearing tribe of the Yanomami. Here
Odin wanted to correct historic imbalances by inverting standard assumptions:

> *It is no longer the theatre which wants to conquer the village, but the village that wants
> to seduce the group, and in this attempt reveals the need for theatre, something of which
> they were ignorant before.*[14]

Their engagements challenged those with whom they bartered with the precondition that such experiences and journeys had also to question, define and so reward the Odin actors.

The rural explorations benefited the actors by giving them an objective perspective on their craft. The alien social environment rid them of their assumptions thereby challenging their role as performers and people. Facing an audience who had little or no experience of any theatre, they could not rush in to educate or attempt to impress them. At first they simply continued to operate as they did every day. Actors relearnt the quality and purpose of work, as their training associated itself with the manual labour of the villagers. In addition to this acid test, barter gave the group resources as they collected local songs and stories. Odin's performances evolved to use diverse theatrical forms as are encountered in villages, including music and parade structures. Use of outdoor spaces and constant reassessment for different ethnic groups and geographical and social situations gave their theatre dynamism and a broad range of forms and styles. In their quest to communicate through performance they selected the most appropriate means to find common understanding. This dynamic can be explored further by examining Peter Brook's 1972 journey to Africa, detailed in John Heilpern's *Conference of the Birds*.[15] This reveals how the participants' naive idealism was harshly undermined by the difficult circumstances. It is beyond the scope of this book to further assess what was a short digression in the many years of Brook's practice.

Barba has moved on from this work in villages to now focus on what he has called Theatre Anthropology.[16] Engaging with experts and theatre practitioners he is following a similar academic line to Grotowski in his Theatre of Sources. In 1979 Barba gave this research external form by founding ISTA — the International School of Theatre Anthropology. This has organised numerous symposia and meetings and has generated much interest in original and Oriental cultural forms. The key aims of ISTA are to enrich acting and training through bringing together artists from disparate cultural backgrounds, to share knowledge and learn in a practical analytical environment. As well as his participation in ISTA's events, Barba directs new performances and is recognised as one of the world's leading innovative directors.

Odin's journeys to villages outwardly seem to have many connections with Gardzienice's own rural work. Both directors started the major part of their creative life under Grotowski, though at very different stages: Barba during his theatrical and Staniewski his paratheatrical period. This is revealed in the emphases they choose. Gardzienice's explorations were initially more ethnically defined than Barba's with their four years of intense Expeditions in Poland. These were more integral to Staniewski's process of rehearsal and performance than to Barba's. To a greater extent than Odin, Gardzienice formulated their performances in villages from material gathered there. This can be clarified by briefly analysing the two companies' corresponding use of textual material.

Odin now place a similar emphasis on the spoken text as Gardzienice put on song. In their early rural journeys in foreign countries words had less importance for Odin because of the language barrier. Gardzienice on the other hand could use dialogue overheard in villages and their spoken and sung texts could be understood by their audiences. In this way the use of Expeditions for Gardzienice's work related to every aspect of their theatrical creative process. It was not primarily training-centered as seems to be the case with Odin, who could more readily separate the experience of their fieldwork from daily rehearsal processes. The corresponding number of Odin's performances is also much higher than Gardzienice's, who have longer gestation periods. This partly echoes the directors' experiences with Grotowski which gave them different priorities, but also the contrasting theatrical cultures in which they operate. For example, rehearsals in post-war Eastern Europe have been notoriously longer than in the West during the same period. In part this is due to fewer commercial pressures. Yet specifically this reveals the important place which Expeditions initially held at the core of Gardzienice's practice.

Another distinction is in the political relevance of the two directors' work, which Barba highlights and Staniewski underplays. Barter pertains to equal relations and respect and for Barba, culture is inseparable from issues of social status and politics. This perhaps stems from the colonial and exploitative imbalances of Western history which he is attempting to address. Barba's concerns are visible in the terminology he uses such as 'barter, ghetto, marginalisation and revolution'. Differences also reveal themselves in the fact that he will organise barter in urban 'floating islands' as well as rural ones with similar pretexts. Although Staniewski also holds urban Gatherings we have seen how these may be considered a separate entity from rural ones. Staniewski is more concerned with culture removed from causality, its background and its functions. For him art is closer to magic and has communicative potential on a spiritual level. He is interested in the social rather than political animal. His terminology shows this by including words such as 'mutuality, alchemy, *genius loci* and the environment'. This difference could be located in the disparity of the formative political and cultural backgrounds of the directors. More tangibly, it has some relation to the environments in which they have established themselves.

Gardzienice live and work in constant close relation to their inspiration and audience, surrounded by Staniewski's 'native culture'. Barba works on the edge of a small town — Holstebro — in Denmark. His is an urban perspective and he must either travel across borders to find 'floating islands' or bring representatives of other groups to him, as he is now doing through ISTA. Gardzienice operate in a more localised context than Barba. Looking for people of a kindred spirit in villages they are stimulated as much in the tensions between high and low culture, as those between ethnically diverse groups. Yet as both Poland and Gardzienice occupy a more central position in Europe, their parameters and objectives are altering. They are heading in a similar direction to Barba, leaving behind the domain of folk and rural arts to focus more on theatrical and festival-based artistic circles. They are now an international theatre resource with their large rural base and perhaps Barba's separation of performances and research may be a possible future form for Gardzienice.

One possible future model is the Japanese Suzuki Company of Toga run by Tadashi Suzuki. He has been dubbed the 'Japanese Grotowski', though he has identified his greater use of texts in part to explain the inappropriateness of this title. He started working in theatre in the 1960s and created an ensemble which he trained by his own rigorous method, which is now taught by some practitioners in America and even practiced by a repertory group there. In 1976 he moved his company to a converted farmhouse in the mountains, 600 kilometres from Tokyo. He was looking for vital sources of energy away from the deprivation and noise of urban life, searching for a home:

> *We need a place that we can always carry in our hearts even when we go elsewhere; we need a place that can serve as a source of inspiration and stimulation.*[17]

The area was suffering from agricultural decline, population loss through migration to cities and cultural devastation. Traditions and long established communal values and practices were being eroded through the isolating influences of television and other technologies and poverty.

The Toga village centre has since been host to numerous international training programmes and theatre meetings and Suzuki has established strong links with American performers. The dormitory space in three accommodation blocks, which can each house up to thirty people, helps defy the seeming isolation of the village. Toga is an hour by car from the city of Toyama but special buses are laid on from there for audiences. Suzuki does not isolate his company in the village. He is now building his seventh theatre and wants to activate a network of theatre spaces outside Tokyo to stress the virtues in decentralising culture. Suzuki is an energetic and highly successful fusion — a shrewd businessman and a devout Romantic visionary.

One can also identify a vivid response to changing external circumstances when Suzuki's oppositional and isolated stance shifted with the country's increased openness, economic expansion and Westernisation. Professor Yasunari Takahashi cited Suzuki's direction of the musical Sweeney Todd in 1981[18] in the commercial Imperial Theatre of Tokyo, as an influential symbol of the increased flexibility of contemporary directors and their role as diplomats, open to international influences. The question of whether Staniewski will follow a comparable path to Suzuki is indeterminable, yet it is one feasible option. To some extent, in their recent mix of Eastern and Western texts and music Gardzienice are approaching Suzuki's avowed eclecticism. Their establishment of a cultural centre which can host many groups could also reflect Suzuki's large scale international festivals. This has previously only been possible on a small scale. In July 1993 the paths of the two directors directly crossed as Gardzienice performed in Toga for the 1993 festival. This affirmed the connections between the two groups.

Some strands of this chapter have directly clarified Gardzienice's practice as well as aesthetics. By understanding the processes of the Odin actors during their journeys to villages we can assume similar patterns in Staniewski's group. Knowing the impermanence of Copeau's rural exploits we can marvel at Staniewski's endeavour. In Gardzienice's instance the Romantic vision of working in harmony with nature is increasingly challenged by technology and the financial demands on art in Poland to pay for itself. Perhaps Suzuki's example of large audiences, a highly developed technological infrastructure and fierce business acumen in a remote mountain village is Gardzience's future model, after this hopefully brief period of economic hardship and reassessment.

8

AN INTERCULTURAL ASSESSMENT

Interculturalism hinges on the questions of autonomy and empowerment. To deploy elements from the symbol system of another culture is a very delicate enterprise. In its crudest terms the question is: when does that usage act as cultural imperialism?[1]

This statement does not serve as a definition of interculturalism, but provides a starting point in highlighting the intricacy of exchanges and influences across ethnic borders. As the world has changed from isolated self-sufficient communities to a complex, economically interconnected and predominantly industrial entity, so have the options open to artists radically transformed. One cannot divorce creativity from questions of history, economics, politics and nationalism. The very expression 'cultural imperialism' shows heightened contemporary understanding of the connection between politics and art.

Recognition can be the first step in negotiating the difficult tightrope which avoids destructive acculturation.[2] Honesty is also imperative to avoid deception and manipulation. Peter Brook has been accused of negative interaction. The director of the San Francisco Mime Troupe, Davis, is one of those accusing him:

> *I am not advocating what Peter Brook does, which is to visit the natives and revamp their culture in the frame of the Great Western European Tradition ripping off multitudes in the wake.*[3]

However one views Brook's work, his good intentions should be remembered even if they were at times naive, as in Africa. Davis' attacking attitude underlines the complexity of intercultural issues for theatre practitioners and the risks when working in such a field. If the extent of the external influence simply involves appropriating ideas and motifs from another system, then this too should be done with deep understanding of the context they come from and the craft that made them.

In reaction to exploitation, principles like Barba's barter and Gardzienice's practice have evolved. Likewise, the role of anthropologists has been questioned for many years. Partly what distinguishes anthropologists and ethical artists from those 'ripping off' is that they believe they can learn from the people they encounter and have no desire to solely manipulate them. They are prepared to earn knowledge by a commitment of time and energy and do not want to sell cheaply the

riches gained from their contacts. Having acquired knowledge, considerate practitioners then integrate this material into their own processes, be it via the
anthropologist's science or the theatre director's art.

Barba and Grotowski were inspired by and transformed the foreign techniques which they encountered in the formative days of the Laboratory's activities. They made them their own and created from them a unique group culture.
This transformation is central to the ethics of responding to diverse ethnic influences and not creating ersatz versions of Oriental art. Schechner has followed their
example, setting guidelines for Americans artists:

> *What's important about these contacts is not the direct taking of Asian ways … but the*
> *adaptation to American circumstances of underlying patterns, the very thought of per-*
> *formance: the master-disciple relationship; the direct manipulation of the body as a means*
> *of transmitting performance knowledge; respect for 'body learning' as distinct from 'head*
> *learning'; also a regard for the performance texts as a braiding of various performance*
> *'languages' none of which can always claim primacy.*[4]

Barba's Theatre Anthropology does not seek the strange or exotic in other cultures,
which predicates a Western, analytical superiority. Rather he is looking to gain
insight into traditions and culture through a comparison of similarities. Barba sees
the process thus:

> *A theatre can … open itself to the experiences of other theatres not in order to mix together*
> *different ways of making performances, but in order to seek out the basic principles which*
> *it has in common with other theatres, and to transmit these principles through its own*
> *experience. In this case, opening to diversity does not necessarily mean falling into syn-*
> *cretism and into a confusion of languages.*[5]

This points to the heart of the ethics of intercultural engagements. Groups meet
each other to gain greater understanding with neither having higher status. There
may be provocation and a clash of cultures and aspirations, but both parties should
be left with enhanced knowledge and benefits. Interaction will lead to change,
whereas exploitation tends to uphold stasis, for what is encountered is plundered
and maintained for one-sided gain.

The ethics of intercultural exchanges and relations are central to
Gardzienice's practice. The company is provocative but avoids exploitation in
Expeditions and rural Gatherings, for the members have little desire to take elements from the cultures with which they interact solely for their own benefit. Their
intention to inspire traditional culture has had equal footing with their own self-
seeking urges and has always been surrounded by reinforcement of the broad value
of 'native culture'. However, this emphasis has shifted as they have moved the
main location of their work from the villages of Poland and their audience has

switched from villagers to international urbanites. The balance which makes interculturalism constructive in terms of meeting, intervention and provocation easily veers towards manipulation and appropriation.

The close connection between economic and artistic values is clearly revealed when considering the perspective of those being exploited. Mining of minerals has been equated with artistic plundering:

> *Music has often been named by Africans and Asians as one of the 'raw materials taken from our part of the world' and processed by a system in which scholars adopt roles that resemble those of other manufacturers and distributors.*[6]

Yet music travels so freely across borders that cross-fertilisations and 'theft' are inevitable. Models such as Barba's or Gardzienice's careful approach are conducted in close relationship with the partner and stimulate cultural activity, making the interaction positive. It is questionable whether these should be equated with 'plundering'. One can however understand the sensitivity of the debate when the significance of music for native peoples is considered.

Songs can have values for native cultures beyond the aesthetic satisfaction with which we in Britain are familiar. For Australian Aborigines, singing is equivalent to the naming of places and objects and has rich metaphysical meaning, as Bruce Chatwin's novel *The Songlines* describes.[7] Songlines are musical maps that define the Aborigines' territories. Music can keep the past alive in the present, providing and perpetuating links with a group's history and identity. Franz Boas was the first of many who have described oral genres as a people's autobiographical[8] ethnography. In eastern Poland religion seems to be a dominant motivating factor that encourages singing. The marginalisation of these communities by the Communist State and the suppression of religion could have activated them in a specific way. The ethnomusicologist Nettl outlined some of these possibilities, without particular reference to Poland, when he wrote that 'One may say in song what one is not permitted to say in speech . . . Music may be an antidote, an expression of anti-culture.'[9] Traditional music, rooted deeply in local history, can prevail against the dominant flow as a strong vehicle for expression. In Poland, folk music was under the auspices of the State and encouraged among national rather than minority groups due to centralist political theories. Sacred music escaped severe external manipulation, but for ethnic minorities the dominance of the Roman Catholic Church undermined their rites and worship. Nettl's observation approaches the heart of why music is the predominant art form encountered in rural areas among the minorities of eastern Poland. It can then be understood why it is central to Gardzienice's practice.

Groups who exist in fragile, marginalised situations place marked value on their own history and self expression:

the roots of traditional cultural patterns still exist and... they may be revived, especially in psychologically difficult or critical situations. This last phenomenon is evidently vital among social groups or individuals living away from their original homes... in all these situations, traditionalism and ethnicity play vital social roles, and they highlight the significance both of folklore and of folk music in particular... peculiarities of performance contribute more than other features to the creation of national or ethnic styles.[10]

Gardzienice want to ensure that small native communities are not consumed by dominant groups and the pervasive trends of pacification, commercialisation and homogenisation of culture and ethnic identity. By then employing folk music in their theatre, they create what could be called a national theatre (as defined in ethnic and not political or geographical terms) that transcends man-made borders to reveal a Slavonic sensibility, that Mickiewicz proposed. This is not exclusive but posits the values of all ethnic groups and is exemplified by their mixture of songs in performance, where a Yiddish lullaby follows a Russian Orthodox hymn. 'Raw' materials are thoroughly cooked by Gardzienice. They transform the music, giving it new qualities and contexts, as Kolankiewicz revealed with his invented term 'ethno-oratorio'.

Barba's academic model of 'Theatre Anthropology' has little connection to Gardzienice's work in villages which could rather be described as 'anthropology for theatre'. However, as they do not set themselves up as anthropologists, they avoid such problems as encouraging villagers to present themselves artificially. The danger of fieldworkers encouraging playacting has been analysed by Schechner in *Between Theatre and Anthropology*.[11] Gardzienice veer away from this partly by practical means: by selecting their team for Expeditions carefully, by keeping numbers limited and by recording songs discreetly. More significantly they prevent false presentations by their methodology in that their meetings are spontaneous and their knowledge is empirically gained. Gardzienice's observation and research is not objective social anthropology, but demands an intimate sharing of space, activities and culture, particularly songs, dances and work patterns. Unlike most anthropologists this takes place over a very short time span. Filipowicz has described this contact from participating in a few Expeditions, detailing their non-prescriptive nature:

Operating on the borderline between theatre and non-theatre, the Gardzienice is not doing missionary work or taking culture to the primitive masses. Neither does it promise salvation to urbanised mankind. Instead its seeks out and follows the earlier tribal modes of social existence based on oral (rather than written) tradition and direct (rather than anonymous) contact in order to discover the essentials of human creativity. When theatre works emerge as a result of the processes they are not tools for instruction or social action but rather an integral and potentially enriching part of living itself.[12]

I will illuminate this conclusion to her article and show how Gardzienice interact with the primary intention of sharing rather than taking, and how the indivisible connection for them between life and theatre makes them not view others' culture in mercantile terms.

It is useful to attempt to ascertain the extent to which rural communities have shaped Gardzienice's practice. One can then see how their interculturalism operates by mixing high and low art as much as it involves alchemy between ethnic groups. Gardzienice's training has developed according to this contact in many ways: by using folk songs; the adoption of unfamiliar physical positions, gestures and vocal inflections; bold, even physical, contact with audiences; various notions such as finishing something abruptly and then moving on to the next thing — not 'celebrating a moment', as Staniewski would describe it, which is always encountered in villagers' singing. Likewise, their performances are short, direct, intense and multi-layered, reflecting the ability of villagers to cross easily from a corporeal to a metaphysical level of perception. These ideas and practices are not copied from villagers directly but have evolved through a pattern of letting people and an environment influence both life and work. Events, objects and rhythms from daily life are reproduced and altered by Gardzienice to then appear in rehearsal or performance.

Beyond this practical application of rural sources in Gardzienice's work, there are still more subtle influences. Their performances are pervaded by a Slavic, emotional spirit. Perhaps more hidden in urban areas, the harsh life in rural regions focuses the intensity of this *Weltanschauung*, revealed most markedly in song:

> *In brief, we can describe the basic Slavonic characteristics as tending towards lyricism and a predominance of emotional qualities ... quite differemt from that of a pure, autonomous system rooted in the causal and linear manner which prevails in European thought most clearly observed in the contrast between Slavonic and Western, especially German music.*[13]

Czekanowska goes on to elaborate technically on this concept, providing a useful distinction. There is a strong sense in rural Slavic culture of often irrational emotional expression and lament linked to the proximity of death and the pervasive presence of church, graveyard and the ghosts of ancestors, as typified in the text of *Dziady*. Gardzienice's performances are full of spirits, religious practices and beliefs, and observations of human vicissitudes. In *Avvakum*, a woman's weeping over a dead body becomes an outburst exposing his drunkeness: '*Pijany jesteś*'she shouts — 'you're drunk'. The transition between lament and laughter, the importance of non-linear narratives and the play of dualities all appear in Gardzienice's works.

Gardzienice harmonise with people rather than manipulate them, as they observe and gather material: 'the group is interested in preserving songs as they are performed by individual folk singers, not in polishing or improving folk materials.'[14] However this does not mean that they are not demanding. Staniewski wants to encourage a clash of cultures and friction to inspire creativity and fuel artistic discoveries. He stresses the need for demands to be made both of his group and of those to whom they travel. He deems it necessary to be provocative, to cut through falsification, pretense and in particular, official fabrications.

Village culture has proved resistant to external impositions but it is eventually effected, as ethnomusicologist William Noll has noted about the area in question:

> Over a short time period of one or two generations, music practices tied to specific contexts often seem able to coexist, without necessarily impinging upon or negating one another. Over a longer period of time, however, certain practices become less context-specific; styles and fashions blend to become a new identity.[15]

Schechner would perhaps argue that such changes are an inevitable part of evolution and development, yet he would also recognise the dangers of manipulating culture for political purposes. Gardzienice search for old (that is pre-Second World War) traditional songs. It might be hard to specifically unearth localised songs because of the urbanisation of the countryside and extensive ethnographic displacement during and after the Second World War but Gardzienice are persistent in their intentions. This is driven by their belief in the imminent death of the cultures they are visiting, an attitude that has been described as 'urgent anthropology',[16] reflecting Levi-Strauss's thinking.

Noll has written about Polish and Ukrainian villages and revealed some of the problems Gardzienice face and trends that they attempt to reverse. They are helped in their task through detailed research and Reconnaissance, to cut through the blurring of urban/rural, geographical and ethnic boundaries:

> notated music and national symbols have converged in several parts of the world over the last few decades to help create what has become a predictable and widespread style of music.[17]

This statement calls to mind Miłosz's words about the great Russian sea in which Stalin wanted to swamp the Soviet and world cultures.[18] Gardzienice reject political manipulation of individuals, promoting self-determination. This demands a constant struggle against the ideological, manipulative invasion of the countryside by urban ideas and people, be they Communist or liberal nationalists, ironically a movement from which Gardzienice cannot themselves be completely separated.

Staniewski wishes to embrace in his creations the contrast between Western and Eastern ways of thought and being, between the Byzantine and Roman
spirit, that Czekanowska alludes to. He has described how among the Slavic people
(presumably especially those of Poland) 'Two elements have mingled here over
the last two centuries... The element of organisation, which was a cross between
Western order (Ordnung) and Eastern Imperialism'.[19] During the Partitions we
saw how Poland was affected by its division between three powers. Staniewski is
looking to discover the Slavic spirit Mickiewicz described, full of excess, contradictions, duality and emotion. Avvakum represents this conflict, vacillating
between high moral values and drunkenness as Staniewski has noted:

> My idea of 'Eurasian' is based on what I've learned from Mickiewicz who still dominates
> our work... Read Dostoyevski to know what I'm talking about. A personality where
> opposites are present simultaneously... In Western society, where personality is deter-
> mined by reason, Avvakkum's behaviour is completely incomprehensible. Maybe that's
> why there are so many complications in East-West politics.[20]

In their travels Gardzienice bridged the two worlds, combining Western tours and
Expeditions with meetings in Polish villages. These contrasts were then distilled
in performance. The last line of Staniewski's statement has however now been
overtaken by political and social events. It will take a long time for influences from
the West to deeply transform the Slavic spirit, particularly in isolated areas, but
changes are already affecting Gardzienice's artistic choices. They have lost contact
with villages and Slavic inspiration in turning towards Celtic and Western culture.
This may unbalance the cultural mix which rooted their original intentions.

By recording village songs and creating an 'ethno-oratorio' from the
gathered material, Gardzienice could be seen to be appropriating cultural gems
from different sources. Songs they use come both from communities they have
visited and artists they have worked with throughout the world. Some are their
own recordings, such as the Russian Orthodox ones that comprised *Avvakum*'s
score, others are not, like the songs from the Codex Burana. Yet in all instances the
music is assimilated and transformed through Gardzienice's vision. Through hours
of rehearsals the original shapes are transmogrified to become rooted in the action
of a performance. Gardzienice positively acknowledge and respect their sources,
taking cautious note of and using original techniques. An assured, authentic base
is then extended. A Georgian song in *Carmina Burana*, reproduced on tape originally by an all male choir, is utilised by the male and female performers of
Gardzienice, synchronal with strenuous acrobatic duets. The mixed sex choir then
adds to the sound. The song is theatricalised and becomes an integrated part of
the performance. Removed from its source, it can be judged merely as a piece of
Gardzienice's art. It is not as objective sham presentation of a cultural artefact but
a resonantly emotive song for Gardzienice. By touching the song's nerve and find-

ing a physical shape for it, they imbue the music with the sort of value it may hold for its original singers.

The company members avoid pretense by openly acknowledging that they do not sing for the same purpose and in the same contexts as the villagers. The group has a different consciousness and most individuals have no religious motivation to sing. They have been to university, travelled and read widely and above all are theatrical artists. Their contact with villagers serves to remind them of the roots of culture and a metaphysical level inhabited by religion and the dead. They are desperate to avoid imitations and falsifications by clearly defining their own presence and nature.

Gardzienice possess vivid cultural and referential foundations in Poland and the Slavic people. Expeditions are for example ethnically more specific than Barba's wider wanderings with his group. Although Barba's theatrical aims are more lucidly presented and documented, Gardzienice's focus on Slavic ethnicity gives their intercultural explorations a purpose and a foundation that stabilises international aspirations. However, they already seem to be operating considerably more on a higher cultural level as Expeditions have become rarer. In building their base in Gardzienice, the company's wandering free-spirited nature, that has defined their individuality outside of conventional patterns, could disappear completely. The balance between a travelling and a producing group has been destabilised, partly simply in order to survive financially. The intercultural nature of Gardzienice's work on terms of this higher/lower axis — the contradiction between two kinds of culture within one ethnic group — previously determined the very nature of all their activities. By distancing themselves too far from this once central ambiguity and by being dominated by modes from a high cultural level, they could lose their identity and become prey to standardisation.

One danger with Expeditions now is that they could approach what I would call 'anthropological tourism', approximating Brook's arguably unethical research, typified in his travels in Africa. If the gain is purely Gardzienice's and performances are not given as part of the barter, then how can the group justify its large presence in the villages? The collection of materials for theatre is then no longer justifiable. How Gardzienice redefine their work in order to avoid such problems is a vital question as tourism becomes established in Poland.

As the Central European territories and former Soviet Republics have opened up with the demise of Communism, economic and artistic exploitation are a big potential danger there. For Western anthropologists this is a vast new area for research. For theatre artists it promises more urban centres on a touring schedule. Yet exchanges and co-operation need not be dominated by the richer and more powerful partner and economics do not have to control culture, as Staniewski indicated by investing in the mill in Gardzienice. Historic awareness can help suggest how intercultural relations should be conducted and may help avoid destructive tendencies of the past. The example of Gardzienice reveals many of the difficult ethics of cultural interaction, made more complex by the rapid changes in Polish society.

9

SEARCHING FOR A NEW LANGUAGE

From Gardzienice's beginning Staniewski consciously built relationships with theoreticians and critics and openly declared his artistic intentions. Since 1990 he has attempted to redefine the group's position, moving from a discussion about a 'new natural environment for theatre' towards a more general debate about 'ecology'. He relates ecology to the idea of finding and settling into a home. Yet Staniewski's desire to describe his group as independent of a social and political context and his desire to control evaluations of the company's work hinder possibilities of a more thorough reappraisal of their position in post-1989 Poland. More open acknowledgement of Gardzienice's present situation would reflect current public priorities and encourage impartial analysis of their work.

The transition towards a market economy has deeply affected the nature of self-advertisement in Poland. The previous State controlled system of arts patronage meant that the money and support a company gained was bureaucratically regulated and could depend on contacts, bribes and political affiliations, as well as quantifiable criteria like location, number of audience reached and their social background. With no necessity for companies to promote themselves competitively in commercial terms, concentration on purely artistic and ideological debates could be fiercer. The fact that Polish theatre and film poster design was internationally celebrated in the 1960s and 1970s shows that within restrictions there was great invention and artistry. Competition amongst Polish directors led to the publication of many manifestos, perhaps most interestingly by Kantor. Even underground groups had a forum in many *samizdat* publications. Artists and politics have been closely interwoven in Eastern Europe in the post-Second World War years. Andrzej Wajda and Vaclav Havel, who have both combined artistic careers with political ones, are but two examples of this proximity. This helped keep the arts in the public eye and fostered respect for artists, which in turn encouraged debate. It was stimulated by factors such as the creation of the four year Theatre Criticism course at the Warsaw Drama Academy.

In keeping with such an artistic ambience, Staniewski introduced his company's ideology to an international audience at a public meeting of the International Theatre Institute in Sofia in 1979. This was through the statement 'For A New Natural Environment for the Theatre' which developed ideas written in his 'Rural Programme'. The latter had been printed locally and distributed informally in Poland. Now such manifestoes cannot avoid being read alongside more commercial treatises. The language of commerce has become widespread and publicly accessible debates have started to enter artistic and once relatively closed domains. Mickiewicz's view of the artist as a *wieszcz* or visionary has been challenged by notions of the artist as both a creative being and a businessman, accountable to a tax-paying public and not just state organisations.

Appraisals of Gardzienice's practice have been proposed in several symposia. Before 1990 they had organised two major international forums: on 'Theatre and Folk Traditions' (1980) and 'The Nature of the Word in Theatre Cultures' (1987). The first was part of the International Theatre Meetings and the second was organised with the cooperation of the International Theatre Institute. Beginning in Autumn 1990 Gardzienice hosted a series of week-long symposia in Gardzienice, twice a year for a three year period. These were targeted at a group of young Poles, had a particular ideological basis as well as a strong connection with Swedish cultural groups. They relied on minimal private sponsorship, money from the British Know How Fund, the British Council and Ministry of Culture backing, and were attended by up to one hundred non-paying guests, most of whom were already familiar with the company's work and were making some contribution to the events.

The function of such symposia are manifold: to highlight and develop Gardzienice's performance work and explorations, focusing them academically and theoretically; to showcase the work of other companies; for Gardzienice both to lead workshops and programme others; to encourage international cooperation by providing a chance for people who work in similar fields to meet; to create models of theatrical activity with a balanced mix of theory and practice; and finally to provide a forum for debate. I will focus my analysis on the three year phase of symposia in which I participated, rather than on the two earlier ones which are only sketchily documented.

A priority of the recent phase of symposia was to focus Gardzienice's work towards young people. This transference of interest arose from Staniewski's concern to transmit the knowledge his group have acquired among older people to younger artists. Their work in villages has often excluded youngsters by virtue of the economic fact that few remain in remote areas. This new focus valorises Gardzienice's experiences by putting them into the hands of those who will have the most enduring use for them. Staniewski also emphasises the value for young people of working in a non-urban rather than urban environment 'where everything is done hastily and superficially. It must guarantee a possibility of concentration and experiencing its environmental values'.[1] This emphasis interlinked the main idea of ecology in the symposia to this specific target group.

The Swedish emphasis in two of the symposia raised questions about the relationship between provinces and centres and encouraged Polish contacts with their Swedish neighbours. Assuming differences in the national characteristics of the respective peoples and simultaneously endorsing these contrasts, Staniewski is searching for points of connection. Gardzienice is a provincial location in Polish and European terms but has become an important national and international theatrical centre. Staniewski notes that Sweden lies outside the central land mass of Europe and in its peripheral role in European economics and politics it is loosely comparable to Poland. In noting these fragile connections one starts to consider Europe in terms of a North-South axis rather than the more familiar East-West one. Present conditions are transitory, as Dziewulska has noted, for Gardzienice is a centre when one thinks in terms of pre-Second World War Poland, which included parts of the Ukraine and if one draws a circle connecting the three major cities of Warsaw, Lvov and Cracow.[2] The term 'centre' was thus theoretically challenged by Staniewski's pronouncements. In discussing this European axial imbalance, Staniewski also stressed the idea that centres are fed by practices formulated in the margins, which highlights the significance of his own achievements.

For Staniewski, joint practical enterprises should be the ultimate aim of symposia. The cooperation with the Swedes, and most directly with Chris Torch of the company Jorgcircus, culminated initially in 1992 in what was called an Expedition to the Baltic island of Gotland off the east coast of Sweden (the Baltic is Poland and Sweden's shared water). The group's activities included open rehearsals, workshops and meetings with local artists. This gave concrete form to one of Staniewski's overriding concerns which is to create an 'unusual alchemical mix of cultures'.[3] Staniewski's responses to Gotland emphasised that the beautiful natural and mythical environment was of inspirational value for Gardzienice. The island is not known for its native culture. It is more renowned for tourism and being home to many rich and famous Swedes, Ingmar Bergman among them. The historical and architectural aspects of the island were therefore more significant to Gardzienice than its living culture. Plans were discussed to one day bring to Gotland Baltic people from different countries, perhaps creating a Baltic cultural centre on the island. Such work is hardly part of an Expedition in the old sense.

There were some clear benefits of symposia organised by an active theatre group rather than a bureaucratic institution. The main focus became practical work, be it workshops led by a selection of international practitioners or Gardzienice themselves, as well as demonstrations by invited experts. There were theoretical discussions and presentations but these happened with a marked emphasis on setting and atmosphere. They occurred according to a set structure or 'harmonogram', but within that there was room for change and developments. Even during symposia Staniewski vigilantly ensured a coherent aesthetic vision, controlling both audience and active participants to that end. Events proceeded with an

organic rhythm, but there was always the presence of Staniewski and the preor-
dained structure to determine the schedule, which was resumed if spontaneity led
to chaos.

The three year programme of symposia and Gardzienice's present phase
of work come under the broad title 'Theatre in Relation to Ecology'. This is ecology in its etymological sense, from the Greek word *'ecos'* or home which relates to
the spirits which such places have. Staniewski has outlined his intentions in this
manifesto:

> *Culture is born from the image that we all have in our hearts of our 'inch of land'. As*
> *artists we are wandering through the world and searching for this 'inch of land' into which*
> *we can inscribe our presence. 'Ecos' in Greek means 'home' while creativity I under-*
> *stand as a dialogue with the spirit (genius loci). Therefore it is necessary to talk about*
> *the ecology of the spirit and through it the ecology of art. With genius loci one can talk*
> *through music and the language of the voice. How is it possible to restore the musicality*
> *and thereby spiritual quality to all forms of theatre work?*[4]

Such an exposition did not lend itself to debate. In bringing together ecology and
theatre Staniewski is making an important connection for his own group's work.
However, the non-Swedish symposia which I attended had vague premises, with
too little time or space given for discussion necessary to come to mutual understanding. They therefore became showcases for Staniewski's theories, presenting
provocations not to be challenged, but ideas to be confirmed or simply reformu-
lated.

As far as can be assessed from written accounts, the 1987 symposium
seemed to have a clearer basis of analysis from concrete and accessible assumptions. It was attended by a highly respected mix of people (incuding Joseph
Chaikin) from a wide range of countries, like Japan, Australia, and Israel. The 1980
symposium had a more general theme but brought together a specifically inter-
related group of participants, who included Barba and E. T. Kirby amongst them.
The more recent symposia have been unfocused and dominated by Europeans,
which points to an important gap in these meetings.

A major aspect of Gardzienice's plans related to their creation of a base in
their village is the idea that it becomes a central meeting place for Eastern and
Western influences. The symposia were meant to foster this fusion of cultures:

> *Gardzienice lies on the fringes of where Cultural Europe meets Cultural Asia. Here, more*
> *than anywhere else, it is possible to conduct activities which return the East back to*
> *European Culture…The borders of the East must open up for the infiltration of spiritual*
> *as well as material culture. In these new times, Gardzienice can be a post where a particu-*
> *lar kind of alchemy of culture may occur.*[5]

Staniewski is trying to redefine the position of Gardzienice as an artistic centre in
a deeply transformed Poland and a post-Cold War Europe. The company's work

was initially based around the notion of travel to encounter other cultures. Now this is being inverted to bring other people to them. This reflects Poland's reforms which are encouraging investment and increased foreign relations. However, the 'East' has so far been poorly represented in symposia, which is probably due to economic and political difficulties. The alchemical reactions can only begin to create sparks if the people exist as elements in the experiment.

One clear part of their revised ethos which reflects and challenges the economic and social reforms is Staniewski's idea to encourage the revival of the local economy. At one end of Gardzienice village there stands the wooden water mill. The company bought this in the winter of 1990. Seventy five percent of the mechanisms were still in working order and were soon repaired with Rodowicz's assistance and the Association's money, mostly gained from performing and training work abroad. For Staniewski the plan to get the mill working has value well beyond practical aid to the village and the reversal of Communist ideological absurdities:

> *A working mill can influence not only the harmony of village life but also should play a principal role as a culturally creative vehicle in itself... Culture is not merely a 'function of economy'. An effort can be made to prove that culture can inspire economic management. It is the last chance in our country to transform the 'heroism of slavery' [Mickiewicz as quoted in* Avvakum — *see page 86, note 15] into the heroism of fruitful work... Our House of Theatre Practices and its surroundings will be an example of such practical ecology.*[6]

In such statements one sees clearly Staniewski's vision. On the first of February 1992 the mill became active again to the delight of many villagers and Staniewski himself. Such concrete practical achievements reveal the actual potential when theory and practice correspond.

Another concrete realisation of a theoretical aim is visible in the regular village performances in Gardzienice village. In 1990 Staniewski wrote:

> *During the next three years we shall start on a series of performances and Gatherings created in this 'Spatium' (i.e. the village)... This recalls the tours which our company undertook some years ago in the great open spaces of Eastern Poland Lappland, or the Appennines, but now resumed and condensed into a single place.*[7]

Like many others, Staniewski has said that he is happier to work in Poland now than ever before because of the absence of Communist restrictions. They are performing occasionally in Polish cities like Cracow, Warsaw and Toruń to which they never took their work before 1989. The company are now 'at home' in Poland, which is recognised in home-grown acclaim if not in the Government's financial assistance. In December 1991 they received a thirty percent cut in Ministry of Culture subsidy; a month later they were heralded as Poland's leading theatre group in the Warsaw Theatre Meetings. The ironies of their success are numerous, underlined by disparities between their intention to work at home and the reality. For at least half of 1992 the company were abroad, responding to invitations to tour and take workshops in Sweden and Great Britain. The necessity to make money to survive these difficult times continues to frustrate their intention to build up their home.

The idea of establishing a substantial base is fundamental to Gardzienice's future development and also a particularly Polish preoccupation. Barańczak has written extensively about the problems of exile and emigration for East European writers.[8] The Polish obsession with exile and the homeland has connections to the lives of the Goliards and wandering artists of the Middle Ages. Marginalised and homeless, they travelled from community to community, their art sharpened by their isolation and detached, nomadic identity. For Staniewski such artists are almost role models, identifying with no-one, operating on the margins of society, able to move between countries and cultures. This inspiration is also important for the Italian Dario Fo.[9] Yet Gardzienice's empathy with the *ordo vagorum* of the Middle Ages is no longer pertinent if their flight has become settlement. By now emphasising the values of their home in the village of Gardzienice, the group seem to be moving away from the tradition to which they belonged and to which they continually referred. Gardzienice are no longer in political or social 'exile' or opposition. Like Barańczak's exiled or emigre writers and like Theatre of the Eighth Day, who are now settled in Poznan, they are tongue-tied by the loss of their former 'native language', which for theatre artists is rooted in the context of their particular public.

The Middle Ages have been a continual reference point for Gardzienice's practice with Staniewski finding enormous theatrical potential in such sources. He has found invaluable the combination of fantasy and action, superstition and agricultural labour, with the body and voice used to their full potential and imagination reaching to its limits. The influence of the Middle Ages is also revealed in the close relationship for Staniewski between theatre and the church and his attempts to revive the *spirit* of theatre, for example by performing in religious or historic buildings. The predominance of icons and images amongst a largely illiterate society has also yielded rich source material which Staniewski has readily translated into theatre. The company thus looks back to the earliest market place events of European drama and a vibrant communal actor/audience relationship.

Arts from the Middle Ages can be connected to still existing folk customs, for many ancient patterns survive in rural folk forms. Gardzienice's practice and their literary and theoretical sources are thus fused in their village meetings. They might quote and refer to the Romantic plays and Mickiewicz's ideals, yet their spirit comes from the lawless celebratory culture of wandering minstrels and jongleurs. Mickiewicz is important for Staniewski because of his nurturing of the

Slavic arts, but as much because he closely entwines material and spiritual worlds in his use of bold imagery and primitive folk rites which still exist in Eastern Poland. Now that Gardzienice's situation has changed so radically, other frames of reference need to be sought in order to equate their practice with the wider context. As the fabric of the countryside develops at a fast pace, ancient practices and patterns of behaviour might disappear altogether. Gardzienice's living source material, (if these villagers and their rituals, beliefs and expression can be so quantified), is being threatened with extinction. These people should not be relegated to perpetual obscurity, isolation and poverty, but the inherent positive qualities of their lives should be recognised and stimulated. The debate about Gardzienice's future must analyse progress as a threat to rural culture.

Staniewski is often mystical in his interpretation of Gardzienice's work. Poor translations add to this problem, as does the speed of social change. Yet in spite of these difficulties, when the marginal becomes central and the village theatre group trains actors at the Royal Shakespeare Company, a more open language needs to be used to reflect the practice. Staniewski is attempting to reposition Gardzienice but I question whether the full implications of this are being acknowledged. This might be deliberate in part to uphold certain Romantic images from the Past: the idea of a wandering, poor, marginalised company is effective currency in the West. Yet the tendency to romanticise verges on the falsehood which paints 'native' culture as exotic. The group which was part of subculture is now forming the main culture, and underground, alternative theories of marginalisation and subversion can no longer be applied to their practice. Technology is radically redefining notions of isolation and the nature of folk culture. Gardzienice may well continue to laud ecological values and organic processes over industrial ones yet the language they use to promote this does not need to stay either in the Middle Ages or in the Romantic era.

CONCLUSION

Gardzienice's practice and the history of their development are inevitably full of contradictions and ambiguities. One complex issue has been their place of work. Gardzienice's travels to Polish villages made their practice deeply imaginative and yet rooted in observation of and immersion in real life — visible in the effects Expeditions had on the literary texts like *Dziady* which they took with them. This book has shown how this 'real life' has changed and Gardzienice have moved away from that process. In 1992, 63 percent of their income came from work abroad. Indispensable though this sum may have been for their survival, it underlined the irony of their decision to root themselves physically in Polish soil. The sheer depth of economic crisis in Poland overshadows all analysis of such complexities and developments.

Gardzienice's turn to the West reflects a broader picture of transformation as Polish cultural trends are influenced by foreign values, imported alongside the slow but steady insurgence of investment. Under Communism, theatre directors had higher ambitions than simply entertaining their audiences. Serious critical statements and veiled comments served audiences' needs more than laughter. Regional theatres now have minimal central subsidy, relying rather on the whims of regional authorities, the support of local audiences and the little private sponsorship that is available, though theatre is most unlikely to attract foreign investment. Directors are more dependent on attracting a paying public, which has made their programming choices less adventurous and ambitious. Light romps were previously infrequently performed but have now ousted both tragedies and classic Polish dramas. One of the more popular plays in Poland since 1989 has been Michael Frayn's *Noises Off*, a British farce. At Warsaw's *Teatr Studio*, a former Communist stronghold and flagship, the Polish production of the Broadway-style musical *Metro* has been hugely popular and profitable, though ticket-prices mean that a seat is a hard-earned luxury. When the producer transferred the production to America's Broadway it flopped after the first week. *Metro* in part gained its status in Poland from the fact that it represented all that was anathema to the former rulers of that country. Using unknown amateur Polish talent it also frightened and annoyed many professional actors, who were used to the former system of salaried long-term contracts.

In spite of such major difficulties as finance, the benefits of the changes should not be overlooked. The increased transmission of Western materials and models is opening up the introverted 'closed circles', exposing them to commercial pressures and energising them. Such developments are healthy in encouraging fresh ideas and access to a broader range of resources, such as private sponsorship and Western funds as well as textual sources. One question inevitably asked is why people should not now laugh if before they could only lament. I would counter this by saying that the Polish people must discover their own comic styles and make their own informed cultural and theatrical choices rather than fawn to mercantile whims, facile entertainment and ready-made cultural artefacts. The influx of influences needs to be regulated and the transition into a freemarket system should be slow and measured rather than fast and externally controlled, as has been happening in Poland. How one filters cultural inspiration and monitors it — without heavy-handed repressive tactics reminiscent of Communism and when commercial cross-fertilisations are deemed so urgently vital — is a question which is being assessed by all involved. This may help avoid an insurgence of the crudest Western concepts and materials.

Fears of the commercialisation of Polish culture are already proving founded. Since 1989 television has transformed its output to include many more pure entertainment and consumer-oriented programmes, with pornography, competitive game shows like the 'Wheel of Fortune' and soap operas. Gauche advertisements for expensive goods unattainable by the greater percentage of Poles are but one highly visible example of this. An English analyst has expressed his fears with specific reference to theatre:

> *Anyone who experienced the excitement of those 'alternative' productions in the claustrophobic context of the ailing Marxist state cannot help being apprehensive about the long-term effects on Polish culture of standing in line; but the queue this time is the one outside the Common Market headquarters, and the price of entry may turn out to be higher than any the Communists could have devised.*[1]

The lure of making money in the short term may obscure long term views. My analysis of attitudes to Romanticism and Romantic dramas suggested some of the losses implicated in knee-jerk reactions. The initial rejection is understandable in light of the history of those texts but it overlooks their value for Polish culture as artistic creations separate from political or nationalistic aspirations. Such foundations need to be reintegrated in fresh ways rather than destroyed by neglect or dismissed for the sake of fickle fashion.

To answer such problems Polish theatre cannot be nostalgic and retrospective, for there are no longer the polarisations which once gave it vigour and focus and which demanded commitment to ideals. However in distancing themselves from Bakhtin, for example, Gardzienice have left behind one central element of his theories of the carnivalesque which provided such an energetic base for theatrical creation: the sense, spirit and joy of rejuvenation. In carnivals the world is turned upside down and opposites meet to then be reborn, recreated or at least redefined. The fusion between this celebration and Slavic lamentation, carnivalesque contradictions, clashes and realignment made Gardzienice's work dramatically tense, demanding and thrilling. This specific presence is diminished in *Carmina Burana*. The dynamics that have replaced the carnivalesque are not yet clearly definable, though the energy of their performances seems now to come less from contradictions and more from an inclusive harmony.

Without social polarisation, the possibility remains of employing other conflicts and tensions within theatrical traditions. Lech Raczak, director of Theatre of the Eighth Day, is perhaps the most reputable spokesperson of the former age, with some objective distance gained during the company's temporary spell in exile in Italy. He is patiently optimistic for Polish theatre yet still points to tensions as vital creative stimuli:

> *The new generation are to be born. The younger groups from the late Seventies...Provisorium, Visual Stage, Gardzienice...it is true that later there is a gap but I believe that in the new social situation we should expect a very different and new theatre and I believe that they will be very much in opposition to our theatre.*[2]

The generations that were artistically nourished by contradiction seem unable to break out of that frame of reference. This points again to the notion that opposition fuels creativity, as seems to have been the case in Poland. Even Gardzienice, who in a rural context distance themselves from official structures and who created performances which did not have a strongly aligned political stance, constantly battled against Communist ideology and ethnic and cultural principles.

We are now witnessing the protracted death of that former age with social transformation filtering into all areas, urban and rural. What Raczak seems to be suggesting for the future is a movement away from the previous theatrical traditions of which he is a figurehead and which have left an indelible and internationally recognised heritage. To interpret him more precisely, he seems to be anticipating not more opposition according to the former model but rather a process of learning and development through rejection of acquired knowledge and experiences: the process characterised in the movement of Vakhtangov away from Stanislavski's teachings or perhaps seen in Staniewski's departure from Grotowski's paratheatre. This may provide a constructive and valuable point of orientation for the young artists who will be creating into the next century, though such groups and tensions do not seem to exist yet.

There may now be hostility to prescriptions and theorising in Poland and increased respect for free-will and impulsiveness, yet the future theatre also needs to be founded on regulated structures and ideology. Adherence solely to free-market tides will not ensure survival in the present environment, which has its own quality of stormy competitiveness — an unknown quantity for many Poles. Communism encouraged artistic excellence, raised the status of culture and promoted the arts, be it purposefully or not and within tight restrictions. It offered many people security, with the State ensuring that everybody had a job, and created bureaucratic organisations to support, spread and foster the arts. At the same time as there were State-sanctioned murders (perhaps the killing of Father Popiełuszko is most clearly remembered) and innumerable overwhelming social problems, there were remarkable theatrical developments like paratheatre and Grotowski's laboratory work. A democratic Capitalist system might encourage individualism and less social and political restrictions, but can be destructive and unsupportive to artists. Violence as a form of protest may be avoided in Poland and some social problems eased, (not forgetting the emergence of others such as mass unemployment and higher crime rates) but is the cultural price to be paid either inevitable or necessary? Again Hyde offers an up-to-date, pertinent outsider's view:

> Freedom of speech is a wonderful thing, but history has never shown any evidence of a necessary relationship between it and creativity. Meanwhile the economy has taken a nose-dive unparalleled since the war. A new 'realism' is in the air; and the issues are no longer so directly political, or expressed so symbolically, or so embedded in the national culture and the mythographic past of Romanticism.[3]

The absence of a clear enemy and the presence of new friends can mean that trivialisations and assumptions arise from confusion. As Barańczak and Miłosz have both often reiterated and as seems the case with Gardzienice, being allowed to speak does not always actuate outpourings of wisdom and insight. Rejection of past foundations does not necessarily lead to stable future growth.

In the eyes of the world, Polish artists profited from their battle with Communist oppression to ultimately prove the victors, though one cannot begin to assess their personal losses. None must underestimate the difficulties of their present situation with its formless nature and vagaries. The fact that the British Government sponsored Know How Fund paid for a British theatre manager and arts administrator, Moss Cooper, to work alongside Staniewski in autumn 1992 was an inevitable sign of progress. This was to help improve their marketing, managerial and administrative practices and assist with their British tour and workshops. Such an arrangement was difficult in practice as one could have anticipated and did little to change Gardzienice's structures. Beyond considerations of mutual understanding and the confused distrust such forced relationships sometimes evoke, what are realistic and feasible alternatives? Is a future scenario for Polish theatre which reflects Western systems inevitable?

My observation of Poland since 1989 may perhaps suggest that transformations have happened only since then, but undercurrents were flowing long before as the birth of Solidarity revealed. Gardzienice could revert back to their former rural practice in Polish villages but they have already travelled too far from this. Social structures and patterns have also altered to such an extent that the 'social vacuum'[4] Nowak described is no longer pertinent terminology; there are now open possibilities to hold informal small-scale meetings. Gardzienice's Gatherings have less significance in a freer society where ethnic rights can be democratically asserted. This fact combined with the new awareness amongst ethnic minorities would have altered the context of their work if they were to tour to Polish villages today. Their performances could revert to being rarely performed for audiences of twenty or thirty in isolated places, yet this would be a closing down and limiting process. It could be argued that Gardzienice's village work might now have a more heightened purpose and potential as open social policies are pursued and former wrongs are publicly redressed. Yet in such a context their practice would not have a provocative role, instead reflecting official trends and following a different set of rules which do not necessarily adhere to Gardzienice's approach or intentions. Other groups may respond to the present conditions, answering the social needs that arise today in remote areas and amongst the ethnic minorities of Poland, perhaps using Gardzienice's ground-breaking fieldwork as a starting point.

A need to locate an audience and talk directly to them in a language they understand and with performances which are particularly crafted for them seems a strong and clear motivation for making theatre. This also seems particularly valuable if that audience is otherwise minimally served in both economic and cultural terms. Small specialised theatre groups who are not confined by pressure to produce performances have a place within any country's cultural make-up, for that is where explorations and advances can be made. The needs of marginalised, isolated audiences must be addressed. This does not now seem to be Gardzienice's role but one for groups that come after them and time, space and money must be given for this in Poland.

If seeking a panoramic vision of the relationship between practice and theory in Gardzienice's history, it is the more public aspects of Gardzienice's practice which have evolved so extensively, leading to inconsistencies in the way they are described. Their Expeditions and Gatherings have become unfocused, particularly when considered in the light of their original qualities and explanation. This seems to also be true of their symposia and the statements which correspond to these, though lack of documentation make this hard to quantify. Gardzienice's training, though, remains challengingly unique with specialised workshops where limited numbers can participate. In these one can touch the raw, spontaneous

energy of Gardzienice and Slavic rural culture. Their village existence still highlights the virtues of a natural environment for the theatre and can be celebrated for
its difference from urban and other familiar structures. However, it has lost some
of its rough spontaneity with its new material edifices — visitors might previously
have been billeted amongst local villagers, whereas now they stay in the restored
oficyna. Their performances have also evolved in that their satirical nature and
provocative tone have faded. *Carmina Burana* is optimistic and embracing rather
than questioning. Perhaps as Christopher Innes[5] has pointed out, such a journey
from satirist to commentator is the usual development of alternative theatre
groups, who are eventually accepted and integrated into the mainstream.
Gardzienice's passage from a national to an international group partly affirms this
claim.

   With this progression, Staniewski now faces challenges of another order.
The burden of managing a larger, older and more unwiedly group, the pressures
of touring, combined with the stresses of sustaining success on the international
festival market, take their toll. To confront these problems and respond to rapid
changes perhaps demands more strength than the previous battle with Communism which had a clear agenda. From the present transitional confusion a clarity
and strength might grow, recalling the heyday of Polish theatre; a period that began with Grotowski's Laboratory and seemed to end with *Avvakum* and
Gardzienice's Expeditions in Polish villages. Gardzienice's artistic practices and
theorising now lack the coherence and purpose they formerly possessed as they
move towards more open structures. It is to be hoped that without the walls the
houses will remain standing in these turbulent times. Theatre is formed in response
to the social and political environment in which it exists. As yet, Gardzienice have
not fully defined their place in contemporary Poland, but the process has begun
and the seeds have been planted.

POSTSCRIPT

The writing of this postscript is strangely timely as observers of Eastern Europe describe the end of a chapter in history and look forward to a new phase of activity. Not only have the former Communists been given majority rule in parliament — in what could be seen to be a backlash against free-market values — but the Polish President has changed. Since his 1990 election as President, Wałęsa's popularity has dwindled — several polls in 1994 proved him less popular than General Jaruzelski, the instigator of Martial Law — and then risen, most noticeably during the November 1995 Presidential election. After a close-fought battle he was replaced as President by the young former Communist Aleksander Kwaśniewski on November 20th 1995. Whatever this new President actually does with his power (in pre-election statements he avowed his commitment to bring Poland into NATO and continue market reforms, though many fear he will actually reverse such policies), political conflicts will certainly endure in a country that was split by the second round of voting (Kwasńiewski gained 52 percent of the vote compared to Wałęsa's 48 percent).

As I hope this book has shown, instability and uncertainty about their future are not new to the Polish people. Since 1993 when my research ended, political and legal confusion has continued to unsettle Polish society. Instability has been fuelled by the fast growth and expansion in the Polish economy, which on a positive note has given a solid base for future economic and political building. The most visible polarities in Polish society are now the contrast between the new super-rich and an ever poorer underclass. Those with money have the luxury of operating within a confused and mostly inoperative legal setting, which is simultaneously unpicking the past and inventing the future.

A full update on Gardzienice's activities until the present time of writing is beyond my reach. I can merely outline certain events and changes, some of which are hinted at in my *TDR* article of Spring 1995 (*TDR* 145) (the research for which was concluded at the end of 1993). Beyond the personnel fluctuations noted in that article, Anna Zubrzycka-Gołaj announced her departure from Gardzienice at a meeting of the Magdalena Project in Cardiff in 1994, stating that what people in Poland now need is food and not theatre. She declared her intention to set up a soup kitchen in Lublin. Catherine Corrigan also left the company in 1994 and returned to Britan. Jadwiga Rodowicz has now moved to Japan and is no longer involved in the company's activities.

Gardzienice have recruited new young members into the company, some of whom participated in a collaborative programme with the Royal Shakespeare Company in January 1995. This also included musical collaborator Maciej Rychły of Kwartet Jorgi and British playwright Howard Brenton. In autumn 1995 these two were both invited to Gardzienice to develop new performance material. The collaboration with the Royal Shakespeare Company has grown from just being a training programme, now possibly leading to a performance of an as yet indeterminate nature. Tony Hill, Project Director of the Other Place who is co-ordinating the British side of the collaboration, explained to me how he is cautious not to impose the demands of a repertoire company on Gardzienice. He is also trying to seek the financial means for such a project, to allow it to happen with as few restrictions as possible. Paying British actors overtime on Equity contracts when they are working throughout the night in Gardzienice does not make sound financial sense. Concrete details about the collaboration should be available by the time this book is published. Whatever the outcome, the process is certainly changing both companies' practices, possibly transforming the use of the written and spoken text in Gardzienice's performances.

Gardzienice's profile as a company offering a high standard of performer training at an international level has grown, with training of Royal Shakespeare Company actors again taking place in 1994. As well as being involved in actor training programmes in America in summer 1995, Staniewski led a four day vocal workshop entitled 'The Art of Dissonance' with Rodowicz and Sadowska in Cardiff in April 1995, organised by the Centre for Performance Research. This was linked to a symposium on the Voice in performance and was one among many vocal workshops.

At home in Poland, Gardzienice's performances have now been seen by a huge public, following the film recording by TV Łódź of *Avvakum* and *Carmina Burana*. These were shown on Polish national television in 1994 to great acclaim and were interspersed by a discussion with Staniewski, Dziewulska and the director of the film. This opened up their work to a wide public (television performances of theatre pieces and plays in Poland have both huge audiences and a reputation for high standards) to an extent which would need years of touring live performances. A film about the company's activities — *For a New Natural Environment For the Theatre*, made by the renowned Jacek Petrycki — he was cameraman on Agnieszka Holland's *Europa, Europa* — was shown in Cracow at the *Stary Teatr* in June 1994 and in Cardiff in April 1995. The decision was also made to no longer perform *Avvakum*. The company are still developing their next performance — based on Apuleius' *The Golden Ass* — but there is no indication when it will be premiered and to what extent the Royal Shakespeare Company collaboration will shape it.

In the village of Gardzienice the *oficyna* is being further upgraded and stands as a monumental edifice of the company's achievements. Its position is still precarious, for it could at any point be taken away from the company who simply rent it from the government. Sadly the mill was burnt down in Spring 1994 by what police believe to be a local arsonist. The full potential of this building scarcely had time to be fulfilled before its swift demise. Another grand building in Gardzienice which Staniewski once hoped to restore into a House of Music has also fallen into irretrievable disrepair. This was formerly the house of *Dziadek* (see cover photograph), friend and mentor to the company, and was my home for seven winter weeks in 1989. Energy and money is instead being put into the *oficyna* and surrounds — the gardens are now being restored to their former glory after years of neglect.

Beyond the selected facts provided here I cannot give a deeper survey of Gardzienice's present activities and programme. Their reputation grows in Britain through those who have met them or the inheritors of their approach. Articles such as mine in *TDR* (and the response this provoked — see letters in *TDR 147*) keep their work discussed in an international forum. There is a brief entry on Gardzienice Theatre as they are mistakenly called in the updated *Oxford Illustrated History of Theatre*, edited by John Russell Brown (OUP, 1995, p. 511). The company's activities are regularly written about in Polish publications with one long article published in *Teatr* in December 1994. This was a transcription of a public conversation between Staniewski and critic Dziewulska in the *Stary Teatr* in June 1994. This revealed Staniewski talking more openly about his sources of inspiration and background (including his relationship with Grotowski) than has previously been documented. It was accompanied by edited conversations between Gardzienice members and Royal Shakespeare Company actors after a two-week-long training programme in December 1992. This was less interesting as it comprised only immediate subjective responses to the training.

Gardzienice village remains an important pilgrimage site for young Poles and many others fascinated by contemporary European theatre practice. Yet Filipowicz's 1995 *TDR* article 'Demythologizing Polish Theatre' suggests a new phase is both imminent and necessary in Poland:

> *The future of Polish theatre does not depend on Kantor, Grotowski, Gardzienice and Eighth Day... Eighth Day, Gardzienice or even Grotowski, for that matter, may still surprise us with a radical departure from their current practices. And Polish theatre will undoubtedly continue to draw on the innovations of Grotowski and Kantor. But it is newcomers, some of them noisy, some of them reclusive, who will shape, as always, the new theatre.*[1]

While we wait for Gardzienice's next performance, growing from their integration of newer members with those more senior, we hope that their inspiration to groups throughout Poland and the world endures. Their continued existence and explorations in a tiny Polish village prove the simple fact that you can make exciting theatre anywhere, if you have conviction and if you call your chosen place home.

November 1995

APPENDIX

Polishing up on the Classics

In December they [the Gardzienice Theatre Association] were in England for five days' closed training for thirteen Royal Shakespeare Company actors ... The Polish group comprised Mariusz Gołaj, Tomasz Rodowicz, Anna Zubrzycka-Gołaj, Dorota Porowska, Grzegorz Bral and musician Elżbieta Podleska, under the artistic directorship of Włodzimierz Staniewski ... straight from the Ukraine and a two-week 'Expedition' ... and brought with them some of the people's rough laughter and untamed Slavic spirit.

The host of this encounter was The Other Place under the management of Tony Hill, with Katie Mitchell's initiative. Tony was not ultimately concerned about the success or failure of the workshop. For him it was an experiment with its own integral value — part of the 'regeneration of the RSC', as he sees one function of The Other Place. By embracing the energetic, demanding and strenuously disciplined training of the Polish company, the troubling lack of physicality in British actors could be given a kickstart. Hill described the search in a typically East European, metaphorical manner of someone fishing, unsure what they will get, but sure in the end to catch something — exchanges often start with language.

I arrived in Stratford towards the end of the process. Intense sessions, shorter by the Gardzienice group's normal standards, had been arranged around the RSC actors' stage appearances ...

The workshop leaders responded sensitively to the situation — the actors' nervousness and the need for them to preserve energy for their performances. I arrived to find a glowing closely-knit group, studiously but lightly pushing their bodies and voices to limits, and letting impulses stretch their imagination. Staniewski had initially found a group of tired and tense actors, near the end of a season, and had opened them. Outside the strain of production they could give themselves into the safe rejuvenating arms of Gardzienice.

The process began as always with song — Georgian, Polish, Ukrainian and historical songs from the thirteenth-century Carmina Burana collection. These were transmitted untechnically by repetition and example ...

The RSC actors had answered the demands well, showing flexibility, concentration and imagination, revelling in the experience. Jane Gurnett, Portia in *Julius Caesar*, described her dancer's training as a limitation because of the control which would not allow her to let go . . . This workshop had opened her to realise what a 'soulless' person she is, though she seemed the opposite of this to me — now the actors were being asked not to adopt stage characters but to reveal the truth from within themselves. Jonathan Cullen, Giovanni in *'Tis Pity She's a Whore*, also talked about the soul in less self-condemning terms: 'Anybody can learn a movement but to get to the soul of the movement is another matter.' The differences wrought in their bodies were subtle, but the change in their language was evident.

A direct meeting of the two theatrical traditions was occasionally explored in the workshop. In one exercise an actor put their legs round the waist of their partner and faced forward, head hanging to the ground. They were then lifted up into the air to fall back down in a rocking motion, centred round the fulcrum of their partner. Shakespearean texts were added to this movement. Familiar words flew from the open throat, and the voice soared as the actor swung through the air. New meanings revealed themselves, perhaps unfaithful to an intellectualised context, but inseparable from the action in that particular moment . . .

Friends and RSC guests, actors and directors were invited to see a demonstration by Gardzienice . . . There were slides of the tiny village of Gardzienice and buildings that the company are restoring, and films of early 'Expeditions' among Polish gypsies; wild scenes of dancing and the open mouths of Gardzienice, filling the barns and cottages with their burning sounds. There were slides of the snowy Carpathians, and then Gardzienice poured into the room — chanting a Ukrainian song, stamping in complex syncopations. This gave way to delicate vocal acrobatic and physical sequences taken from their new performance *Carmina Burana*. Two pigeons met and cooed together, embracing in a physical dance. They played a love scene from the story of Tristan and Isolde in which the love-birds are courting . . . The RSC actors supported them with their voices and then a pigeon stepped forward from amongst them . . .

Tony Hill is sure Gardzienice will soon return to work there with a larger group. Staniewski is just as keen for a relationship to develop as he lightheartedly revealed: 'In two weeks we would make a performance.' Such a small private beginning should grow into a fuller more sustained relationship. Then perhaps Adrian Noble, who reacted with great enthusiasm to the demonstration and the actors' responses, can ask with some justification: 'Can we afford the candle bill?'

(Adapted from *The Stage and Television Today*, 9 January 1992)

NOTES

Abbreviations used in the notes and bibliography include: CPR — Centre for Performance Research, CUP — Cambridge University Press, OUP — Oxford University Press, PAJ — Performing Arts Journal, TDR — The Drama Review (formerly Tulane Drama Review), NTQ — New Theatre Quarterly, MIT — Massachusetts Institute of Technology.

INTRODUCTION

1. Tadeusz Kantor quoted in 'Storming the Palace' in *The Independent*. An article by Thomas Sutcliffe, Arts Editor. 23 February 1990.
2. Bakhtin, Mikhail *Rabelais and his World* translated by Helene Iswolsky. MIT, Massachusetts, 1968.
3. Innes, Christopher *Holy Theatre* CUP, Cambridge, 1981. p. 241
4. Barańczak, Stanislaw *Breathing Under Water* Harvard University Press, London, 1990. p. 16. (His next collection of essays is to be called *Choking on Air*, reflecting on later events.)
5. Miłosz, Czesław *The Captive Mind* Penguin, Harmondsworth, 1980 (first edition 1953). p. 75
6. Coplan, David in 'The Meaning of Tradition' in *Ethnomusicology and Modern Music History* edited by Stephen Blum, Philip Bohlman and Daniel Neuman. University of Illinois Press, Chicago, 1991. p. 40

CHAPTER 1

1. See the map of the Partitions.
2. Mickiewicz, Adam *TDR* Vol. 30, No. 3, T 111 Lesson 16 'Slavic Drama' delivered in 1843, translated with an introduction by Daniel Gerould. MIT Press, London, Fall 1986. p. 94
3. ibid. p. 96

4. Dernalowicz, Maria *Adam Mickiewicz* Interpress Publishers, Warsaw, 1981. p. 61

5. The 'Great Emigration' led up to and included the effects of the November insurrection of 1830. It describes the mass exodus of Polish people to safety in the West and their flight from oppression. It resulted in Paris becoming the Polish 'capital' in the mid 1800s.

6. Gerould, Daniel in his introduction to Lesson 16 'Slavic Drama' *TDR* Vol. 30, No. 3, T 111. MIT Press, London, Fall 1986. p. 92

7. Jerzy Grotowski quoted in *Grotowski's Laboratory* edited by Osiński and Burzyński. Interpress, Warsaw, 1979. p. 86

8. Nowa Huta was a purpose-built town for steel workers in the region, who comprised a large percentage of Szajna's audience. A factory and dwelling complex, it was created by the Communists after the Second World War to dilute the troublesome influence of the intellectuals in Cracow. This ploy backfired and Nowa Huta has repeatedly been the scene for violent demonstrations against the authorities. The pollution from the factories there sweeps over Cracow, eroding its historic buildings.

9. 'The Word Unheard: "Form" in Modern Polish Drama' by George Hyde explains how these three practitioners' visions have influenced Polish directors. *Word and Image* Magazine Vol. 4, No. 3/4 Taylor and Francis Ltd, London, July–December 1988.

10. 'Cricot' is an inversion of *To circ* which in Polish means — 'That's circus'. Cricot was the name of a pre-war surrealist cabaret group in Cracow which inspired Kantor.

11. Miłosz's *The Captive Mind* gives detailed insight into how this imposition of style affected writers and led to simultaneous official and unofficial existences — see the chapter entitled 'Ketman'. Penguin, Harmondsworth, 1980.

12. Official guidelines paraphrased in *The Contemporary Polish Theatre* by Edward Csato. Interpress Publishers, Warsaw, 1968. pp. 23–24

13. *Poland — A Handbook* An essay entitled 'Development and Dissemination of Culture' by Włodzimierz Sandecki. Interpress, Warsaw, 1974. p. 456

14. Halecki, O. and Polonsky, A. *A History of Poland* Routledge, London, 1990. p. 348

15. Kott, Jan *Theatre Notebook, 1947–1967* Garden City, New York, 1968. pp. 50–51

16. Csato, Edward *The Contemporary Polish Theatre* Interpress, Warsaw, 1968. p. 32

17. Gerould, Daniel *Twentieth Century Polish Avant-Garde Drama* Cornell University Press, London, 1977. p. 94

18. Tymicki, Jerzy An essay entitled 'New Dignity — The Polish Theatre 1970–1985'. *TDR* Vol. 30, No. 3, T 111. MIT Press, London, Fall 1986, pp. 27–28

19. Cywińska, Izabella From a speech called *The Culture of a Little Bit of Ground* presented in November 1991 at The British Council, London, on an official visit. Recorded by myself. Cywińska's 1981 production of *The Accused of June 1956* at Poznan's *Teatr Nowy* was a direct reference to the more than fifty workers killed by the authorities during demonstrations in Poznan. For this production and her support of Solidarity she was imprisoned on the first night of Martial Law. She is now head of the *Fundacja Kultury* which is a private arts funding body.

20. Prus, Maciej quoted in Bożena Kowszewicz's article entitled 'Theatre In Crisis: Exit Audience' in *The Warsaw Voice* a weekly newspaper in English. Polish Interpress Agency, 17 March 1991, Warsaw. p. 10

CHAPTER 2

1. Fire, John (Lame Deer) 'The Meaning of Everyday Objects' an essay collected in *Symposium of the Whole — A Range of Discourses towards an Ethnopoetics* edited by Jerome and Diana Rothenburg. This book is on Staniewski's private bookshelf. University of California Press, London, 1983. p. 171

2. Staniewski in the CPR Booklet from 'For a New Natural Environment for Theatre' Cardiff, 1989. p. 13

3. Wiktor Herer and Władysław Sadowski elaborate on this idea in the chapter entitled 'The Incompatibility of System and Culture and the Polish Crisis' in *Polish Paradoxes*. Routledge, London, 1990. p. 125

4. 1 hectare = 10,000 sq. metres. The average Polish farm in 1958 was six hectares according to S. H. Franklin in *The European Peasantry*. Dover Publications, New York, 1958.

5. The Arians were named after the fourth century Greek heretic Arius. They were a radical Protestant sect which seceded from the Calvinists in 1569–70 to advocate a primitive Christianity and were the forerunners of the Unitarian church.

6. Franklin, S. *The European Peasantry* Dover Publications, New York, 1958. p. 209

7. Davies, Norman *God's Playground — A History of Poland* Clarendon Press, Oxford, 1981.

8. See *Sex, Dissidence and Damnation: Minority groups in the Middle Ages* by Jeffrey Richards. Routledge, London, 1990.

9. All numbers are estimates and come from *Contemporary Poland* magazine, No. 12. Factual essay entitled 'Ethnic Minorities in Poland'. Interpress, Warsaw, 1990.

10. Miłosz, Czesław *The Captive Mind* Penguin, Harmondsworth, 1980 (First Edition 1953). p. 231
11. Unknown researcher quoted in Trevor Beeson's *Discretion and Valour: Religious Conditions in Russia and Eastern Europe*. Fontana, Glasgow, 1974. p. 163
12. ibid. p. 86

CHAPTER 3

1. White, Anne *De-Stalinization and the House of Culture (Declining State Control over Leisure in the USSR, Poland and Hungary 1953–89)*. Routledge, London, 1990. p. 45
2. ibid. p. 57
3. *Polish Paradoxes* edited by Stanislaw Gomulka and Antony Polonsky. Routledge, London, 1990.
4. Wedel, Janine 'The Ties that Bind in Polish Society' ibid. p. 240
5. Kolankiewicz and Lewis, *Poland* Pinter Publishers, London, 1988. p. 159
6. Wedel, Janine 'The Ties that Bind in Polish Society' in op. cit. *Polish Paradoxes* p. 255
7. op. cit. *Poland* p. 160
8. Christopher Hann gives a full account of this relationship in *A Village Without Solidarity*. Yale University Press, London, 1985.
9. Staniewski, Włodzimierz in 'Expeditions into Culture' by Halina Filipowicz. *TDR* Vol. 27, No. 1, T 97. MIT Press, London, Spring 1983. p. 56
10. Stallybrass, Peter and Allon White, *The Politics and Poetics of Transgression* Methuen, London, 1986. p. 16
11. ibid. p. 16
12. Bakhtin, Mikhail *Rabelais and his World* MIT Press, Massachusetts, 1968. p. 403
13. ibid. p. 269
14. Staniewski, Włodzimierz in the CPR Booklet from an interview with Richard Schechner. Cardiff, 1989. p. 17
15. Staniewski, Włodzimierz from a statement at a conference in Dartington, April 1989. The conference was entitled 'Performance, Nature, Culture' and was organised by the CPR. The notion of the 'singular truth' is Bakhtin's which he expounds upon in *Rabelais and his World*. MIT, Massachusetts, 1965.
16. Staniewski, Włodzimierz from the CPR Booklet Cardiff, 1989. p. 20
17. ibid. p. 14 Originally from 'For a New Natural Environment for the Theatre'.
18. See articles by Pawluczuk 'The Expedition' (*Dialog* No. 6. Translator unknown. RSW — Prasa Książka Ruch, Warsaw 1980.) Osiński in *Theatre in Poland*

(Nos. 2, 3, 4 Authors' Agency, Warsaw, 1983.) and Filipowicz's 'Expeditions into Culture'. (*TDR* Vol. 27, No. 1, T 97. MIT Press, London, Spring 1983.)

19. Young, Marjorie B. 'The Bernardine Pilgrimage' *TDR* No. 3 T 75 Vol. 21 MIT Press, London, September 1977. p. 37

20. Bakhtin, Mikhail *Rabelais and his World* MIT Press, Massachusetts, 1968. p. 7

21. Polish Sociologist Stefan Nowak created this well known expression in an essay '*System Wartości Społeczeństwa Polskiego* / The Value System of Polish Society' in *Studia Socjologiczne* 4: 75 (1979). It is quoted by Janine Wedel in 'The Ties that Bind in Polish Society' in *Polish Paradoxes*, edited by Stanislaw Gomulka and Antony Polonsky, Routledge, London, 1990. p. 240

22. Gołaj, Mariusz from an unpublished interview with Vera Lustig, editor of *Plays and Players*, witnessed by myself. Exeter, 20 June 1990.

23. This figure was cited by Leszek Balcerowicz at a lecture in Senate House, London University for the School of Slavonic and East European Studies. 27 November 1992.

24. Pirie, Donald in the introduction to *Polish Realities*. Third Eye Centre, Glasgow, 1991. p. 19

25. The militia is the name of the police force. In the summer of 1990 their name was changed from '*Milicja*' to '*Policja*' to try to shake off their bad reputation and present a new public face.

26. Skwara, Anita 'Between Social Realism and Romanticism: on the Theoretical Non-existence of Popular Cinema in Poland' An unpublished essay presented at a Warwick University film conference. September, 1989.

CHAPTER 4

1. Staniewski, Włodzimierz CPR Booklet Cardiff, 1989. p. 18

2. I have discovered no explanation of this name other than the fact that it stands for STUdent theatre which in Polish has the same beginning — *STUdencki*.

3. Puzyna, Konstanty *Polityka* No. 4 1971 RSW — Prasa Książka Ruch, Warsaw.

4. Szybist, Maciej 'In the World's Circus'. An essay in *Teatr STU* entitled 'Musicality'. The translation is my own. Młodzieżowa Agencja Wydawnicza, Warsaw, 1982. pp. 53–54

5. *Towards a Poor Theatre* Edited by Eugenio Barba. Methuen, London, 1969.

6. Osiński, Zbigniew *Grotowski's Laboratory* Co-edited with Burzyński. Interpress Publishers, Warsaw, 1979. p. 87

7. Burzyński, Tadeusz 'Grotowski's Exit From Theatre' in *Theatre in Poland* 1975 No. 7 Authors' Agency, Warsaw. pp. 15–16

8. op. cit. *Grotowski's Laboratory* p. 107

9. Jerzy Grotowski in Zbigniew Osiński's *Grotowski and his Laboratory*. PAJ Publications, New York, 1986. p. 140

10. Flaszen, Ludwik 'Conversation with Ludwik Flaszen' (reported by Eric Forsythe) in *Educational Theatre Journal*. Vol. 30/3 American Theatre Association, Washington DC, 1978. pp. 301–328

11. Grotowski, Jerzy '*Via negativa*' — 'not a collection of skills but an eradication of blocks' in *Towards a Poor Theatre* edited by Eugenio Barba. Methuen, London. 1969. p. 17

12. For a highly critical review of a 'Beehive' workshop see Daniel Cashman's 'Grotowski; His Twentieth Anniversary' in *Theatre Journal*. University and College Theatre Association, Washington DC, December 1979. pp. 460–466

13. Jerzy Grotowski from the introductory paragraph of *Holiday — The Day that is Holy*. TDR Vol. 7, No. 2, 1973. MIT Press, London. It is difficult to select one passage to describe all the activities and objectives of paratheatre.

14. *On the Road to Active Culture* edited by Leszek Kolankiewicz. Wroclaw, 1978. pp. 80–82. Originally from Weinstein, Steven 'Wroclaw, the Paratheatrical Experiment: Two Experiences' in *Alternative Theatre*, Baltimore, March/April 1976.

15. *On the Road to Active Culture* edited by Leszek Kolankiewicz. Privately distributed. Wroclaw, 1978. p. 86

16. Staniewski, Włodzimierz CPR Booklet but originally from 'For a New Natural Environment for Theatre'. Cardiff, 1989. p. 13

17. See Richard Mennen's article on a Special Project in America and the detailed preparations for this. *TDR* Vol. 19, 1975, No. 4. MIT Press, London. pp. 61–62

18. Cieslak's 'total act' towards the end of the *The Constant Prince* was claimed to be a crystallisation of Grotowski's intentions. 'A sort of psychic illumination emanates from the actor. I cannot find any other definition. In the culminating moments of the role, everything that is technique is as though illuminated from within, light, literally imponderable . . . He is in a state of grace.' Josef Kelera quoted in *Towards a Poor Theatre*. There is no page number. Methuen, London, 1969.

19. Grotowski, Jerzy quoted in Jennifer Kumiega's *Grotowski*. Methuen, London, 1987. p. 162

20. Staniewski from an interview with Schechner. CPR Booklet Cardiff, 1989. p. 18

21. op. cit. *Grotowski* p. 204

22. Shank, Theodore *American Alternative Theatre* Macmillan, London, 1982. p. 2

CHAPTER 5

1. Staniewski, Włodzimierz CPR Booklet Cardiff, 1989. p. 17
2. *'Dawno temu w Gardzienicach'* by Mariusz Gołaj in *Konteksty — Anthropologia, Kultura — Etnografia, Sztuka* Instytut Sztuki, Warsaw, 1991.
3. Staniewski, Włodzimierz CPR Booklet Cardiff, 1980. p. 18
4. See my article 'Gardzienice: a Village, a Theatre, Crossroads' in *NTQ* Vol. VIII No. 29 Feb 1992. CUP, Cambridge, 1992. p. 51
5. Artaud, Antonin *Theatre and its Double* Calder and Boyars Ltd., London, 1974. pp. 88–95
6. Kott, Jan from an essay 'After Grotowski: the End of the Impossible Theatre' in *The Theatre of Essence*. Northwestern University Press, Evanston, 1984. p. 152
7. Knapp, Bettina L. *Antonin Artaud — Man of Vision* Discus Books, New York, 1971. p. 141
8. Lutz, Dick and Mary *The Running Indians* Dimi Press, Oregon, 1989. p. 21
9. *'Dawno temu w Gardzienicach'* by Mariusz Gołaj in *Konteksty — Anthropologia, Kultura — Etnografia, Sztuka* Instytut Sztuki, Warsaw, 1991. The translation is my own. p. 55
10. ibid. p. 55
11. ibid. p. 55
12. Van Gennep, Arnold *Rites of Passage* Chicago University Press, Chicago, 1960.
13. Schechner, Richard *Between Theatre and Anthropology* University of Pennsylvania Press, Pennsylvania, 1985. p. 19
14. Staniewski, Włodzimierz CPR Booklet Cardiff, 1989. p. 17
15. Albert Lloyd the British folk music expert in Barry Gavin's film *The Miraculous Circumstance*, which traces Bartok's journey in Slovakia, Hungary and Romania. Directed by Barry Gavin for Third Eye Films, 1976.
16. Staniewski, Włodzimierz CPR Booklet Cardiff, 1989. p. 17
17. Bakhtin, Mikhail The title of a chapter in *Rabelais and his World*. MIT, Massachusetts, 1965.
18. A chapter in ibid.
19. ibid. p. 26
20. Many training methods emphasise the use of the pelvis, belly (or *hara* as it is known in Japan) for energising movement, reflecting the influence of the Orient on actor training.
21. *'Dawno temu w Gardzienicach'* by Mariusz Gołaj in *Konteksty — Anthropologia, Kultura — Etnografia, Sztuka* My translation. Instytut Sztuki, Warsaw, 1991. p. 55
22. op. cit. *Rabelais and his World* p. 255
23. ibid. Bakhtin is describing the psychological effects on the individual of immersion in a crowd. p. 256

24. Staniewski, Włodzimierz CPR Booklet Cardiff, 1989. p. 16

25. From unpublished notes by Katie Mitchell, a British theatre director, who visited Gardzienice for two weeks in February 1990.

26. Staniewski, Włodzimierz quoted in Filipowicz's 'Expedition into Culture' *TDR* Vol. 27 No. 1. T97. MIT Press, London, Spring 1983. p. 59

CHAPTER 6

1. 'Ethno-oratorio' was first used in a paper given at the Gardzienice conference of 1987, printed in the CPR Booklet. These quotations come from this paper. Cardiff, 1989. p. 10

2. *'Dawno temu w Gardzienicach'* by Mariusz Gołaj in *Konteksty — Anthropologia, Kultura — Etnografia, Sztuka* My translation. Instytut Sztuki, Warsaw, 1991. p. 55

3. Osiński, Zbigniew 'More than a Theatre' An article in *Theatre in Poland*. Authors' Agency, Warsaw, 1980. p. 22

4. Filipowicz, Halina 'Gardzienice: a Polish Expedition to Baltimore' *TDR* No. 1, Spring 1987. MIT Press, London. pp. 62–63

5. Bakhtin, Mikhail *Rabelais and his World* MIT, Massachusetts, 1995. pp. 187–188

6. Pawluczuk, Włodzimierz 'The Expedition' An article in *Dialog* No. 6. Translator unknown. RSW — Prasa Książka Ruch, Warsaw, 1980.

7. Filipowicz, Halina 'Expedition into Culture' *TDR* Vol. 27 No. 1 Spring 1983, T97. MIT Press, London. pp. 66–67

8. Osiński, Zbigniew 'Sorcery in Gardzienice' *Theatre in Poland* No. 2, Authors' Agency, Warsaw, 1982. p. 20

9. Filipowicz, Halina 'Expedition into Culture' *TDR* Vol. 27 No. 1 Spring 1983, T97. MIT Press, London.

10. Filipowicz, Halina 'Gardzienice: a Polish Expedition to Baltimore' *TDR* No. 1, Spring 1987. MIT Press, London.

11. ibid. p. 142

12. Osiński, Zbigniew 'Gardzienice — The Scandinavian Experience' *Theatre in Poland* Nos. 2–3–4 Authors' Agency, Warsaw, 1983. p. 84

13. Osiński, Zbigniew 'Sorcery in Gardzienice' *Theatre in Poland* No. 2 Authors' Agency, Warsaw, 1982. p. 21

14. Filipowicz, Halina 'Gardzienice: a Polish Expedition to Baltimore' *TDR* No. 1, Spring 1987. MIT Press, London. p. 148

15. Mickiewicz, Adam *Digression to Dziady: Part Three* Unpublished translation by Timothy Dalton. Lublin, 1980.

16. Staniewski Włodzimierz from an unpublished 'Memorial Statement'. Lublin, 1991.

17. Filipowicz, Halina 'Gardzienice: a Polish Expedition to Baltimore' *TDR* No. 1, Spring 1987. MIT Press, London. p. 153

18. ibid. p. 162

19. Bok-Kun, Jun A Korean critic from *Seoul Daily News* August 23, 1988. Unknown translator.

20. As noted from a performance of *Carmina Burana*. Gardzienice, 1991. My translation.

21. See Jung's essay 'On The Psychology of the Trickster-Figure' in *Four Archetypes*. Ark Publications, London, 1972.

22. Bedier, J. *Tristan and Isolde* in a translation by Hillaire Belloc. Allen and Unwin, London, 1936.

23. Kolankiewicz, Leszek 'Gardzienice: the Essentials'. Article from an unknown source, used in the programme for Warsaw Theatre Meetings 1992.

24. Majcherek, Janusz 'Between East and West' in *Gazeta Wyborcza* Warsaw, 2.2.92. He is also editor of *Teatr* magazine.

25. Staniewski, Włodzimierz CPR Booklet Cardiff, 1989. p. 16

26. Staniewski, Włodzimierz quoted in Marek Zagańczyk's 'Between the East and West' in *Theatre in Poland* No. 5. Authors' Agency, Warsaw, 1991. pp. 6–8

27. Zagańczyk in ibid. p. 6

28. Hubner, Zygmunt in 'The Professional's Guilty Conscience: a Letter from Poland' written in September 1986 printed in *NTQ* No. 15. Vol. IV. CUP, Cambridge, August 1988. p. 222

CHAPTER 7

1. *Evgeny Vakhtangov* compiled by Lyubov Vendrovskaya and Galina Kaptereva. From his notebook written in a sanatorium in 1921. Progress Publishers, Moscow, 1982. p. 158

2. ibid. p. 142 From his notebook written in 1919.

3. Carter, Huntly *The New Spirit in the Russian Theatre* Brentano's, London, 1929. p. 183

4. op. cit. *Evgeny Vakhtangov* p. 132

5. ibid. p. 130

6. Rudlin, John *Jacques Copeau* CUP, Cambridge, 1986. p. 10

7. ibid. p. 108

8. ibid. p. 28

9. ibid. p. 195

10. ibid. p. 133

11. This expression comes from Eugenio Barba's *The Floating Islands*. Thomsens Bogtrykkin, Holsteboro, Denmark, 1979.

12. Barba, Eugenio from an interview with Stig Krabbe Barfoed for Danish television, given in Rome 1974. Printed in *Beyond the Floating Islands* by Eugenio Barba. PAJ Publications, New York, 1985. p. 159

13. ibid. p. 160

14. ibid. p. 170

15. Heilpern, John *Conference of the Birds* Methuen, London, 1989.

16. 'Theatre Anthropology is the study of the behaviour of the human being when it uses its physical and mental presence in an organised performance situation and according to principles which are different from those used in daily life. This extra-daily use of the body is what is called a technique.' Barba in his and Nicola Savarese's *The Secret Art of the Performer — A Dictionary of Theatre Anthropology*. Routledge, London, 1991. p. 5

17. Suzuki, Tadashi *The Way of Acting* Theatre Communications Group, New York, 1985. pp. 85–87

18. The point was made during the symposium 'East Meets West: Japan' at the Institute of Contemporary Arts, London. 4.10.91.

CHAPTER 8

1. Chin, Daryl *Interculturalism, Postmodernism, Pluralism* PAJ 33/34, Vol. XI No. 3. 1990. PAJ Publications, New York. p. 168

2. Weber, Carl *AC/TC Currents of Theatrical Exchange* PAJ 33/34. PAJ Publications, New York, 1990. p. 19 Acculturation has been described as 'contagion', the 'first step in assimilation' and a 'process of uniting or the integrating of the patterns of life of two different cultural groups on a somewhat equal basis'. These are by three authors quoted in *Definitions in Sociology* by V. A. Tomovic. Diliton Publications Inc., Ontario, 1979. p. 1

3. Davis, R. G. 'Deep Culture: Thoughts on Third World Theatre' *NTQ*, No. 24 Vol. 6. CUP, Cambridge. Nov. 1990. p. 338

4. Schechner, Richard *Between Theatre and Anthropology* University of Pennsylvania Press, Philadelphia, 1985. p. 23

5. ibid. p. 257 Eugenio Barba quoted by Schechner. Originally from *The Way of Opposites*, an essay printed in *Canadian Theatre Review* 35. (Summer): 12/37. University of Toronto Press, Toronto.

6. Al-e Ahmad from *Gharbzadegi* (Tehran, 1962) quoted by Blum in *Ethnomusicology and Modern Music History* edited by Stephen Blum, Philip Bohlman and Daniel Neuman. University of Illinois Press, Chicago, 1991. p. 3

7. Chatwin, Bruce *The Songlines* Picador, London, 1988.

8. Franz Boas's work *Tsimshian Mythology* (Washington DC, Government Printing Office, 1916. Bureau of American Ethnology, Annual Report 31) is cited by David Coplan in 'The Meaning of Tradition' in *Ethnomusicology and Modern Music History* edited by Stephen Blum, Philip Bohlman and Daniel Neuman. University of Illinois Press, Chicago, 1991. p. 47

9. Nettl, Bruno *The Study of Ethnomusicology: Twenty Nine Issues and Concepts* University of Illinois Press, Chicago, 1983. p. 182

10. Czekanowska, Anna *Polish Folk Music* CUP, Cambridge, 1990. p. 111

11. Schechner, Richard *Between Theatre and Anthropology* See the chapter 'Restoration of Behaviour'. University of Pennsylvania Press, Philadelphia, 1985.

12. Filipowicz, Halina 'Expedition into Culture' *TDR* Vol. 27, No 1, Spring 1983, T 97. MIT Press, London. p. 71

13. Czekanowska, Anna *Polish Folk Music* CUP, Cambridge, 1990. pp. 38–39

14. Filipowicz, Halina 'Expedition into Culture' *TDR* Vol. 27, No. 1, Spring 1983, T 97. MIT Press, London. p. 68

15. Noll, William in a chapter entitled 'Music Institutions and National Consciousness among Polish and Ukrainian Peasants' in *Ethnomusicology and Modern Music History* edited by Stephen Blum, Philip Bohlman and Daniel Neuman. University of Illinois Press, Chicago, 1991. p. 156

16. The notion of 'urgent anthropology' was cited by Bruno Nettl with no source reference but it seems to be unfamiliar jargon for a familiar belief in the pressing need to protect and record dying cultures.

17. Noll, William in a chapter entitled 'Music Institutions and National Consciousness among Polish and Ukrainian Peasants' in *Ethnomusicology and Modern Music History* edited by Stephen Blum, Philip Bohlman and Daniel Neuman. University of Illinois Press, Chicago, 1991. p. 156

18. The Miłosz quotation is note 10, page 26.

19. From press information prepared for the 1986 performances in America entitled 'The Essentials about Gardzienice' originally from Staniewski's 'For A New Natural Environment for Theatre'. p. 2

20. Staniewski, Włodzimierz CPR Booklet Cardiff, 1989. p. 17

CHAPTER 9

1. Staniewski, Włodzimierz from a Memorial Statement written in Lublin, 1991, parts of which (though not this section) were published in *NTQ* No. 29 Vol. VIII. CUP, Cambridge, Feb. 1992.

2. op. cit. *'W Gardzienicach* / In Gardzienice' *Teatr* Nr. 2 Feb. 1991, Warsaw.

3. Staniewski, Włodzimierz from an unpublished section of the Memorial Statement. Lublin, 1991.
4. op. cit. Memorial Statement *NTQ* p. 52
5. op. cit. Memorial Statement *NTQ* p. 50
6. Staniewski, Włodzimierz from an unpublished section of the Memorial Statement. Lublin, 1991.
7. op. cit. Memorial Statement *NTQ* p. 56
8. See Barańczak, Stanisław *Breathing Under Water* Harvard University Press, London, 1990. p. 238
9. See Mitchell, Tony *Dario Fo — People's Court Jester* Methuen, London, 1984, pp. 10–12

CONCLUSION

1. Hyde, George in the Poland section of *European Theatre: 1960–1990*. Routledge, London, 1992. p. 215
2. Lech Raczak in an after production discussion at the Institute of Contemporary Arts, London when they were performing *No Man's Land* (1990). 18.9.92. Recorded by myself.
3. Hyde, George in the Poland Section of *European Theatre: 1960–1990*. Routledge, London, 1992. p. 214
4. See chapter 3, note 21.
5. See page 2, note 3 in the introduction.

POSTSCRIPT

1. Filipowicz, Halina 'Demythologizing Polish Theatre' *TDR* Vol. 39 No. 1 T 145 Spring 1995. MIT Press, London. p. 125

BIBLIOGRAPHY

Artaud, Antonin *The Theatre and its Double* Calder and Boyars Ltd, London, 1974.

Avvakum, Protopop *The Life of the Archpriest Avvakum by Himself* Hogarth Press, London, 1924.

Bakhtin, Mikhail *Rabelais and his World* Trans. Helene Iswolsky MIT, Massachusetts, 1965.

Barańczak, Stanisław *Breathing under Water and other East European Essays* Harvard University Press, 1990.

Barba, Eugenio and Nicola Savarese, Editors of *A Dictionary of Theatre Anthropology: The Secret Art of the Performer* Routledge, London, 1991.

Barba, Eugenio *Beyond the Floating Island* PAJ, New York, 1986.

Barba, Eugenio *The Floating Island* Thomsens Bogtrykkin, Holstebro, Denmark, 1979.

Barba, Eugenio, Editor *Towards a Poor Theatre* Methuen, London, 1969.

Bedier, Joseph *Tristan and Isolde* Allen and Unwin, London, 1936.

Beeson, Trevor *Discretion and Valour: Religious Conditions in Russia and Eastern Europe* Fontana, London, 1974.

Blum, Bohlman and Neuman, *Ethnomusicology and Modern Music History* University of Illinois Press, Chicago, 1991.

Braun, Edward *The Director and the Stage* Methuen, London, 1982.

Bristol, Michael D. *Carnival and Theatre* Routledge, London, 1989.

Brook Peter *A Theatrical Casebook* Compiled by David Williams Methuen, London, 1988.

Brumberg, A., Editor *Poland: Genesis of a Revolution* Vintage Books, New York, 1983.

Bujak, Adam *Misteria* Wydawnictwo 'Sport i Turystyka', Warsaw, 1990.

Carrel, Christopher Donald Pirie and Jekaterina Young, Editors *Polish Realities: The Arts in Poland 1980–1989* Third Eye Centre, Glasgow, 1990.

Carter, Huntly *The New Spirit in the Russian Theatre* Brentano's, London, 1929.

Chatwin, Bruce *The Songlines* Picador, London, 1987.

Chudzinski, Edward and Tadeusz Nyczek *Teatr STU* Młodzieżowa Agencja Wydawnicza, Warsaw, 1982.

Clark, Katerina and Michael Holquist *Mikhail Bakhtin* Harvard University Press, 1984.

Craig, Mary *The Crystal Spirit: Lech Walesa and his Poland* Hodder and Stoughton, London, 1986.

Csato, Edward *The Contemporary Polish Theatre* Interpress Publishers, Warsaw, 1968.

Csato, Edward *The Polish Theatre* Polonia, Warsaw, 1963.

Czekanowska, Anna *Polish Folk Music* CUP, Cambridge, 1990.

Czerwinski, E. J. *Contemporary Polish Theatre and Drama (1956–1984)* Greenwood Press, New York, 1988.

Davies, Norman *God's Playground — A History of Poland* Clarendon Press, Oxford, 1981.

Dernalowicz, Maria *Adam Mickiewicz* Interpress Publishers, Warsaw, 1981.

Drozdowski, Bohdan, Editor *Twentieth Century Polish Theatre* John Calder Ltd, London, 1979.

Evgeny Vakhtangov Writings and articles compiled by L. Vendrovskaya and G. Kaptereva. Progress Publishers, Moscow, 1982.

Franklin, S. H. *The European Peasantry* Dover Publications, New York, 1958.

Gerould, Daniel, Editor *Twentieth-Century Polish Avant-Garde Drama* Cornell University Press, 1977.

Gomulka, Stanislaw and Antony Polonsky, Editors *Polish Paradoxes* Routledge, London, 1990.

Jerzy Grotowski, Workcentre of Document about his activities in French, Italian and English including an essay 'Performer' by Grotowski. No editor cited. Produced by the Centro per la Sperimentazione e la Ricerca Teatrale, Pontedera, 1989.

Halecki, Oscar and Polonsky, Antony *A History of Poland* Routledge, London, 1970.

Hann, Chris *A Village Without Solidarity* Yale University Press, 1985.

Haraszti, Miklos *The Velvet Prison: Artists under State Socialism* Penguin, London, 1987.

Heilpern, John *Conference of the Birds* Methuen, London, 1989.

Hirschkop, Ken and David Shepherd *Bakhtin and Cultural Theory* Manchester University Press, Manchester, 1989.

Innes, Christopher *Holy Theatre* CUP, Cambridge, 1981.

Itzin, Catherine *Stages in the Revolution* Methuen, London, 1980.

Ivanov, V. Editor of *Carnival* A collection of essays including Umberto Eco's 'The Frames of Comic Freedom' and Monica Rector's 'Esscolas-de-Samba'. Mouton Publishers, Berlin, 1984.

Jung, C. G. *Four Archetypes* Ark Paperbacks, London, 1986.

Kantor, Tadeusz *Wielopole, Wielopole* Marion Boyars, London, 1990.

Karpinski, Maciej *The Theatre of Andrzej Wajda* CUP, Cambridge, 1989.

Knapp, Bettina L. *Antonin Artaud: Man of Vision* Discus Books, New York, 1971.

Kolankiewicz, L. *On The Road to Active Culture* Unpublished collection of papers. Wroclaw, 1978.

Kott, Jan, Editor *Four Decades of Polish Essays* Northwestern University Press, Illinois, 1990.

Kott, Jan *Theatre Notebook — 1947–1967* Garden City, New York, 1968.

Kott, Jan *Theatre of Essence and other Essays* Northwestern University Press, Evanston, 1984.

Kumiega, Jennifer *Grotowski* Methuen, London, 1987.

Lane, Christel *The Rites of Rulers* CUP, Cambridge, 1981.

Lewis, Paul and George Kolankiewicz, Editors *Poland — Politics, Economics and Society* Pinter Publishers, London, 1988.

Lutz, Dick and Mary *The Running Indians — the Tarahumara of Mexico* Dimi Press, Oregon, 1989.

Macshane, Denis *Solidarity* Spokesman, Nottingham, 1981.

Marianca, Bonnie and Gautam Dasgupta, Editors *Interculturalism and Performance* Writings from PAJ. PAJ Publications, New York, 1991.

Mackiewicz, Adam *Poems* Trans. George Rapall Noyes. Polish Institute of Arts and Sciences in America, New York, 1944.

Miłosz, Czesław *The Captive Mind* Penguin, Harmondsworth, 1980 (first pub. 1953).

Mitchell, Tony *Dario Fo: People's Court Jester* Methuen, London, 1984.

Nettl, Bruno *The Study of Ethnomusicology: Twenty-Nine Issues and Concepts* University of Illinois Press, Chicago, 1983.

Nietzsche, Friedrich *The Birth of Tragedy* Vintage Books, New York, 1967.

Osiński, Zbigniew *Grotowski and his Laboratory* PAJ, New York, 1986.

Osiński, Zbigniew and Tadeusz Burzyński *Grotowski's Laboratory* Interpress Publishers, Warsaw, 1979.

Paul, Norman H. and John Rudlin *Copeau: Texts on Theatre* Routledge, London, 1990

Pavis, Patrice *Theatre at the Crossroads of Culture* Routledge, London, 1992.

Poland: A Handbook A collection of essays and information Interpress Publishers, Warsaw, 1974.

Richards, Jeffrey *Sex, Dissidence and Damnation: Minority Groups in the Middle Ages* Routledge, London, 1990.

Rothenberg D. and J. Editors *Symposium of the Whole* University of California Press, 1983.

Rudlin, John *Jacques Copeau* CUP, Cambridge, 1986.

Saint-Denis, Michel *Training for the Theatre* Theatre Arts Books, New York, 1982.

Schechner, Richard *Between Theatre and Anthropology* University of Pennsylvania Press, Pennsylvania, 1985.

SCOT — Suzuki Company of Toga A handbook published by SCOT. Tokyo, 1985.

Segel, Harold B. *Polish Romantic Drama* Cornell University Press, 1977. New edition Harwood Academic, Amsterdam, 1997.

Shanin, Teodor Editor *Peasant Societies* Essay 'Peasant Traditional Culture' by Kazimierz Dobrowolski. Penguin, London, 1971.

Shank, Theodore *American Alternative Theatre* Macmillan, London, 1982.

Singer, Isaac Bashevis *The Magician of Lublin* Penguin, Harmondsworth, 1960.

Stallybrass, Peter and Allon White, *The Politics and Poetics of Transgression* Methuen, London, 1986.

Suzuki, Tadashi *The Way of Acting* Theatre Communications Group, New York, 1986.

Teatr STU No editor cited. Młodziezowa Agencja Wydawnicza, Warsaw, 1982.

Thomson, George *Aeschylus and Athens* Lawrenc and Wishart, London, 1941.

Tomaszewski, Jerzy *The Socialist Regimes of East Central Europe* Routledge, London, 1989.

Turner, Victor *Dramas, Fields and Metaphor: Symbolic Action in Human Society* Cornell University Press, 1974.

Turner, Victor *The Anthropology of Performance* PAJ, New York, 1986.

Turner, Victor *The Ritual Process: Structure and Anti-Structure* Routledge and Kegan Paul, London, 1969.

Van Gennep, Arnold *Rites of Passage* University of Chicago, Chicago, 1960.

Ware, Timothy *The Orthodox Church* Penguin, Harmondsworth, 1963.

White, Anne *De-Stalinisation and the House of Culture* Routledge, London, 1990.

Yarrow, Ralph, Editor *European Theatre: 1960–1990* Routledge, London, 1992.

JOURNALS AND MAGAZINES

A short selection of the major articles consulted.

CPR booklet for Gardzienice's United Kingdom tour, 1989 — Cardiff, 1989. This includes, amongst other items, an interview with Staniewski by Richard Schechner which also appears in *TDR* No. 1 Spring 1987, and Staniewski's paper 'A New Natural Environment for the Theatre'.

Konteksty — Anthropologia, Kultura — Etnografia, Sztuka Nr. 3/4 (215) 1991 Polska Akademia Nauk Instytut Sztuki, Warsaw.

Modern Drama Vol. XXVII No. 1 University of Toronto, 1984. 'Theatre of Eastern Europe' Issue.

New Theatre Quarterly Edited by Clive Barker and Simon Trussler. Vol. 8 No. 29 February 1992. Vol. IV No. 15 August 1988. Vol. VIII No. 29, February 1992. Vol. VI No. 24. November 1990. CUP, Cambridge.

Performing Arts Journal: No. 38 Vol. XIII Special Polish Theatre Section. May 1991 PAJ Publications, Baltimore. Vol. II No. 3, No. 33/34 PAJ Publications, Baltimore. No. 17 Articles on Tadashi Suzuki. PAJ Publications, New York, 1983.

Staniewski, Włodzimierz *Gardzienice, Poland* edited by Peter Hulton. Arts Archives, Arts Documentation Unit, Exeter, 1993.

Theatre In Poland Nos. 2, 3, 4 1983. No. 2 1980. No. 2 1982. No. 5 1991. No. 7 1975. Authors' Agency, Warsaw.

The Drama Review: Edited by Richard Schechner. Vol. 7 No. 2 1973. Vol. 19 No. 4 1975. Vol. 21 No. 3 T 75 September 1977. Vol. 27 No. 1 T 97 Spring 1983. Vol. 30 No. 3 T 111 Fall 1986 Poland issue. Vol. 31 No. 1 Spring 1987 Vol. 39 No. 1 T 145 Spring 1995 MIT Press.

The Independent Arts Section edited by Thomas Sutcliffe, 23 February 1990.

The Guardian 2 November 1992, London.

Gazeta Wyborcza 2 February 1992, Warsaw.

Życie Warszawy 9 May 1991, Warsaw.

Twórczość / Creativity RSW, Prasa Książka Ruch, Warsaw, October 1959.

Dialog No. 6 RSW, Prasa Książka Ruch, Warsaw, 1980.

Polityka No. 4 RSW, Prasa Książka Ruch, Warsaw, 1971.

Alternative Theatre Baltimore, March/April, 1976.

Theatre Journal University and College Theatre Association, Washington DC, Dec. 1979.

Teatr Edited by Janusz Majcherek. June 1989, Warsaw, Nr. 2 Feb. 1991, Warsaw.

Word and Image Vol. 4. No. 3/4, Taylor and Francis Ltd, London, 1988.

INDEX

Other titles in the Contemporary Theatre Studies series: